Giant Book of BREAD MACHINE RECIPES

Norman A. Garrett

MAIN STREET

10 9 8 7 6 5 4 3 2 1

Published In 2000 by Sterling Publishing Company, Inc.
387 Park Avenue South, New York, N.Y. 10016

Material in this collection was adapted from
Favorite Bread Machine Recipes

Great Bread Machine Recipes

Quick & Delicious Bread Machine Recipes

Specialty Breads in Your Bread Machine

Distributed in Canada by Sterling Publishing
c/o Canadian Manda Group
One Atlantic Avenue, Suite 105
Toronto, Ontario, Canada M6K 3E7

Distributed in Great Britain and Europe by Cassell PLC
Wellington House, 125 Strand
London WC2R 0BB, United Kingdom

Distributed in Australia by Capricorn Link (Australia) Pty Ltd.
P.O. Box 6651, Baulkham Hills, Business Centre,
NSW 2153, Australia

Manufactured in the United States of America.

Sterling ISBN 0-8069-4793-4

CONTENTS

BREADS YOU FINISH YOURSELF

AMERICAN PIONEER BREADS

SPECIALTY BREADS For 2-POUND MACHINES

BASIC BREADS

FESTIVE BREADS

GETTING TO KNOW YOUR BREAD MAKER

BASIC OPERATIONS

Although bread machines come in various shapes, sizes, capacities, and capabilities, they all share common characteristics and principles of operation. They are all designed to make bread making easy, quick, and complete. Except for placing the proper ingredients in the baking pan, pressing a few buttons, and removing the bread when it is finished (and slicing it, of course), the machine does all the work.

After ingredients are placed in the pan and you start the machine, the following cycles are completed:

1. The initial mix cycle
2. The first rise
3. The "punch down"
4. The second rise
5. The bake
6. The cool down

The length of each cycle depends on the make and model of your machine. Some machines skip the second rise and bake after the first rise. Other machines have alternater settings that let you select a double or single rise (often called the "quick bread" cycle). Some of the new machines have cycles especially created for whole grain breads, which generally require longer rising cycles. In addition, some machines have added capabilities, such as special cycles for cooking rice, jam, quick breads (batter breads), and cakes.

Whatever your machine's configuration, you need to become familiar with the way it works so you can tap its full potential for making delicious loaves of bread.

CAPACITIES AND LIMITATIONS

Each machine has a maximum capacity and limitation. Capacities are usually either 1 pound or $1\frac{1}{2}$ pounds, with a few machines accommodating loaf sizes of 2 pounds. It is not wise to exceed the rated capacity of your machine, because overloading the machine can cause motor damage or dough overflows.

I have seen ads for machines that can bake "3 pound loaves," but the fine print will usually reveal that this will only work in the case of a dense bread that doesn't rise much. I would not recommend baking loaves much larger than your machine can handle, as it could cause damage to your machine, particularly the mixing motor.

What about baking a loaf smaller than the rated capacity? On most machines, that will work fine. The recipes in this book are presented in 1 pound, $1\frac{1}{2}$ pound, and 2 pound sizes. If you have a 1 pound machine, limit yourself to baking the 1 pound loaves. If you have a larger capacity machine, feel free to try both 1 and $1\frac{1}{2}$ pound recipe sizes.

Table 1 shows the basic capacity differences among bread machines currently on the market. You can determine the capacity of your machine from the owner's manual or by checking the white bread recipe that came with the machine. If the recipe calls for 2 cups of bread flour, you have a 1 pound machine. If it calls for 3 or more cups, you have a $1\frac{1}{2}$ pound (or greater) capacity machine.

TABLE 1
BREAD MACHINE CAPACITIES: Basic White Bread Recipe

FLOUR AMOUNT	1 POUND	11/2 PONDS	11/2+ POUNDS
2 cups	X		
2.5 cups	X		
3 cups		X	
3.5 cups			X
3 to 4 cups			X

Note: Determine the amount of flour called for in the basic white bread recipe for your machine. This chart will tell you the capacity of your machine based on that amount. If you do not have access to the basic white bread recipe that came with your machine, assume that it has a 1 pound capacity.

BAKING THE DOUGH YOURSELF

All machines let you bake the dough yourself in the oven by extracting it from the machine after the first rise is complete. If your machine has a dough setting, it will beep when it is time to remove the dough. You can then punch the dough down, knead it, place it in a bread pan or on a cookie sheet for a final rise, and bake in an oven, rather than in the machine itself.

ADDING INGREDIENTS

Some machines have a "mix bread" setting, which will beep when it is time to add raisins, seeds, or other ingredients to the dough. Since not all machines have this capability, I have developed the recipes in this book so all ingredients can be placed in the pan in the beginning. However, if you have a "mix" cycle, alternatively use that cycle, particularly in the recipes calling for seeds, nuts, or raisins. The advantage to adding these ingredients in a mix cycle is that the machine will tend to pound them less in the mixing process. Raisins, for example, will be more likely to remain whole when added in the mix bread cycle.

The timing of rising cycles varies somewhat from machine to machine. Some of the newer machines have separate cycles for whole wheat bread, which extends the rising time for the bread, giving a better rising loaf. Still other machines are programmable, allowing you to determine rise time yourself.

CRUSTS

The baking times vary on bread machines. Most machines offer you the option of selecting the darkness of your crust. The control for this will usually determine the baking temperature of your bread, and will not alter the length of the baking cycle. Selecting darker crusts will cause the bread to bake hotter. I found when using one machine, for example, that turning the dial to the lightest crust setting actually caused some breads to have uncooked dough in the middle. It will probably take a few loaves for you to determine the optimum setting to accommodate both your machine's capabilities and your personal tastes. Once you determine that setting, make a note of it, because you will probably want to bake all of your loaves with that same setting.

KNOWING YOUR OWN MACHINE

You will need to get used to your particular machine. In testing for my books I have found considerable variations among the different machines I have used. You will need to become familiar with two parts of the baking process as they apply to your specific machine: the optimum consistency of your dough and the sound of your machine as it goes through the cycles.

DOUGH CONSISTENCY

Dough consistency, and each machine's ability to deal with different dough consistencies, is important and varies greatly. Some machines will use a runnier dough (more liquid content); others have powerful motors that can easily handle stiffer doughs. Observe your bread as it is mixed. Make a mental note of the dough consistency. Then, when the bread is finished, note the texture of the bread. Learn to compare the finished texture to the consistency of the dough. Soon, you will be able to accurately predict the texture of the bread by looking at the dough immediately after mixing. This skill is important if you want to make any recipe modifications.

MACHINE SOUNDS

As you use your machine, also not the typical sounds it makes as it progresses through its various cycles. If you become familiar with the "normal" sounds, you will be aware when the motor is being overworked and the sounds the machine is making are unusual, which may indicate a process is potentially damaging.

SERVICE AND CLEANING

CLEANING

If you want consistently good bread from your machine, make sure it remains clean. Taking two or three minutes after each loaf has baked to clean the machine will yield consistently better loaves and will assure that your machine stays in peak operating condition.

How hard a machine is to clean depends on its design. Some machines use a bucket with the beater drive mechanism built in. Consequently, cleaning is simply a matter of removing the bread from the bucket, removing the beater, and cleaning the bucket with warm water. On other machines, the beater drive mechanism is not part of the bucket and must be cleaned after each use. This cleaning is more difficult and sometimes results in crumbs in the bottom of the baking chamber. To clean crumbs from the baking chamber, I have found that a damp kitchen washcloth will pick up most of them. I have tried mini-vacuums, canned air, and other methods such as turning the whole unit upside down and shaking it, but I find the simple washcloth the best (and least messy).

All machines have a special nonstick surface in the bread pan. Take care with this surface. Do not use any abrasive cleaners or scouring pads on the inside of the bread pan, or you will damage the nonstick surface. Try not to pry stuck breads with knives, forks, or other hard objects that may scratch the surface. If you must pry, use a rubber or soft plastic device of some kind, like a rubber spatula. If you take care of your bread pan, it will give you many future loaves of bread.

The machines that have the beater mechanism designed into the housing, rather than the bread bucket, also have a small plastic washer. Take great care with this washer. Don't lose it, and rinse it off and dry it after each loaf of bread. Without this washer, you will not have a good seal between your bucket and the bottom of your baking chamber, and leakage will result.

If you have an accident with your bread (such as dough overflow or another big mess), wait until the machine cools down, and take your time cleaning it. Most baked-on bread can be removed with warm water, and that is the recommended cleanup. I have had my share of disasters, but have managed to clean all of them up without even having to use any soap. Simple warm water and a washcloth have always been all that is needed.

LOST AND DAMAGED PARTS

There are generally no user-serviceable components in the bread machine, other than the standard cleaning of the parts just mentioned. However, there are parts that are easily lost or damaged that you can replace yourself. Most prominent on that list is the mixer beater. Since it is a small, removable part, it is easily misplaced. Make sure that you replace the beater in the bucket after each cleaning; that will minimize its potential for being lost.

On machines in which a plastic washer fits beneath the bread bucket, the washer will wear out over time. It is important to keep it clean, and it might not be a bad idea to order a replacement to have on hand, since it is an inexpensive item.

BREAD PAN

The other major removable component is the bread pan. The most likely place of damage is its nonstick surface. If its surface is damaged to the point where bread is sticking to it, replace the bread pan. If small scratches seem to have no negative effect on your being able to remove the bread from the pan, you have probably not damaged the surface enough to worry about it.

MAJOR REPAIRS

If any other problems arise with your machine, it is likely it will have to be sent in for repair. The control panel, for example, will sometimes cease to function and will need to be replaced. You should obtain an estimate of repairs before authorizing any major repairs on your machine because it is possible that the cost of repairs will exceed the cost of the machine, especially since the price of new machines will continue to fall for the foreseeable future as manufacturers achieve economy of scale. The likelihood is that your machine will have a long, productive life, and that it will give you many hours of trouble-free bread baking if you will simply keep it clean and ready for the next loaf.

TROUBLESHOOTING GUIDE

There are numerous variables that can affect your bread. Those listed below are all problems I have experienced while making bread. You may also encounter some not listed here. Before you write off the bread machine completely, send it out to repair, or blame the recipe, think the problem through and make sure that you have accounted for all other possible reasons for the problem. That would include crust settings, proper baking cycles, measuring ingredients properly, using fresh ingredients, checking for power outages during baking (which may recycle your machine), and, finally, curious children pushing buttons.

STUCK DOUGH BEATER

If your dough beater is difficult to remove after baking a loaf of bread, try using some shortening on the shaft before installing the beater, and place dry ingredients in the pan first. In the machines where the beater is self-contained in the pan, soak the beater in water for a few minutes after removing the bread. In some types of machines, the beater will stay with the loaf of bread. In those types of machines, the beater is rarely a problem to remove.

LEAKAGE OF LIQUID

This might be a problem on the machines whose pans have a hole in the bottom to accommodate the dough beater. If you have this kind of machine, place the dry ingredients in the bread pan first. Liquids should be added last. Also, check to make sure you have the rubber sealing washer in the proper position before locking the pan in place, and then make sure the pan is securely locked before adding ingredients.

RECIPE FLOP

Make sure you have added the proper quantities of ingredients. It is easy to become distracted while setting up a recipe and miscount your ingredients. Also, check to make sure you chose the correct settings when baking the bread. Finally, be sure your ingredients are fresh and that the proper type of ingredient has been used. A frequent culprit in recipe flops is yeast that is not fresh.

LOAF-SIZE VARIATION

The size of your loaf will vary according to the ingredients. Although the weight of two loaves of bread may be the same, their size and appearance may vary greatly due to the different ingredients used. In general, breads using gluten-rich bread flour will rise more than breads using flours with less gluten content. Rye breads, for example, will be small, with dense texture, and will bake with a darker crust. The loaf sizes of the recipes in this book refer to weight, not to finished size.

SPOILED INGREDIENTS

The two ingredients you must be cautious with are fresh eggs and fresh milk. Do not use either of these ingredients in a "delay bake" cycle (available on some machines), where you set the timer to start the bread at a later time. Milk would be all right if the delay were not more than an hour or two, but I would not recommend that eggs be used in any recipe that will not immediately be started. If you want to use a recipe calling for eggs on a delay bake, consider using powdered eggs instead of fresh eggs. If you want to use milk in a delayed recipe, use dry milk and add the proper amount of water to compensate.

COLLAPSING DOUGH

If your dough collapses, it probably rose to long. Since the timer cycles are not programmable on many machines, you may consider reducing the yeast by $^1/_2$ teaspoon to get less rising. You also should check to make sure that the machine was not recycled during the process. Recycling can occur from brief power outages, or from children (or curious adults) pressing machine buttons. If a power outage occurs and you are aware of it, you can remove the dough from the machine and finish the process by hand, baking the bread in the oven. If your machine is programmable, set the rise cycle for a shorter time the next time you bake the recipe.

STRONG YEAST FLAVOR

It is possible that too much yeast was added. Cut the yeast down by $^1/_2$ teaspoon and try again.

FAILURE TO RISE

This can be a complex problem with many possible causes. Any of the following will contribute to a loaf not properly rising:

- Using flour with low gluten content (pure rye flour, wheat flour, etc.
- Too much salt in the recipe. Salt is a yeast inhibitor.
- Too little sugar in the recipe. Sugar feeds yeast and promotes rising.
- Yeast is old. Yeast expires. Check your yeast supply and make sure you are using fresh yeast. Old yeast will not activate and rise properly.
- Yeast is dead. This may be caused by adding hot ingredients. For example, if your recipe calls for some ingredients to be boiled before being added to the mix, do not add them until they have had time to cool. Adding ingredients that are too hot will kill your yeast.

UNEVEN TOP

This usually indicates too little liquid in the recipe, but on some breads, such as rye breads, where less rising takes place, this may be a normal occurrence.

COLLAPSED TOP

This is usually caused by too much liquid in the recipe. Cut the liquid back by two tablespoons and try again. Be careful not to make your bread dough too stiff, however, as some machines have underpowered motors that will not be able to handle stiffer dough, particularly in the 1½ pound recipes. Also be aware that some recipes use ingredients that are going to add liquid to the dough during the baking cycle, and a collapsed top might be normal. I found that breads using fresh cheeses generally fall into this category.

RANCID TASTE

Check your whole grain ingredients. Whole grain flours, wheat germ, and similar ingredients should be kept in the freezer. They spoil rapidly when left at room temperature. White flours are not subject to the same type of spoilage and can be left in the cupboard for storage.

WHITE SPOTS

These are from flour that has stuck to the side of the pan during the mixing process and has not mixed into the dough. This problem seems to occur more frequently in square pans than in round ones. When the bread rises and bakes, this flour sticks to the outside of the loaf. While not a taste problem, spots can present a cosmetic problem. The solution is to look into the baking pan after the mixing has taken place. If there is flour stuck to the sides of the pan, take a rubber spatula, remove it from the sides, and mix it in with the dough.

SOGGY CRUST

You left the bread in the pan too long after the baking cycle completed. Some machines have cooling cycles that cool the bread and help remove the moisture. Soggy crust is not as great a problem on these machines, but it is still a good idea to remove the bread and place it on a cooling rack as soon as the final beep is heard.

IMPROPER MIX

This happened to me one time when I had forgotten to replace the dough beater after cleanup from the previous loaf. My solution to this is now to watch the initial mix for a minute or so when I first turn the machine on. I can see the mixing taking place. If the motor is running, but no mixing is happening, check your dough beater. If it has been left out, stop the machine, replace the beater, and start the cycle over.

INCONSISTENT SIZE AND TEXTURE

If you bake the same recipe and get different results, blame the weather. Weather is actually a large factor in baking, as temperature and humidity have substantial control over the amount of dough rising that will take place. Make notes as you bake and you will soon learn to make seasonal adjustments for your particular climate.

LOST DOUGH BEATER

Check the last loaf of bread, particularly if your machine is of the variety where the beater stays in the loaf of bread when it is removed from the baking pan. I had a loaf of bread ready to give to a friend for testing, only to realize that I was about to give away the dough beater too! Get in the habit of cleaning your pan right away and putting everything back in the machine, and your beater will always be where you want it: In the pan, ready to bake.

CONVERTING EXISTING RECIPES

After you have had time to get used to your bread machine, you will probably want to try out some of your favorite bread recipes. When you look at them, however, you will notice that they were not designed to work in a bread machine. Practically any yeast bread recipe can be converted to work in your bread machine as long as you want to go to the effort of making the conversion. The key is to make sure the recipe is yeast-based. Although today we enjoy yeast which is reliable and easy to use, this is a relatively recent development. Recipes that are over 40 or 50 years old will likely use a chemical, rather than an organic, leavening. Chemical leavenings include baking soda and baking powder, and they do not have the same properties as yeast. Do not attempt to convert recipes that are not yeast-based for use in your bread machine.

Some machines have a cycle for "quick breads." These cycles are specifically designed for non-yeast baking (in fact, some machines can even bake cake too!). Often called "batter breads," quick breads are breads that use batter with a consistency similar to pancake batter or cake batter. Quick breads are raised by means other than yeast. However, since most bread machines do not have these cycles, discussions regarding quick bread recipes are really beyond the scope of this book. We will stick to only yeast breads here.

Converting a standard bread recipe to work in your machine is not difficult, but is computationally intensive work, so have a calculator handy if you want to attempt a conversion. A sheet or two of paper will also be necessary, so you can write down the totals and the new, converted recipe.

This chapter will take you through the steps for converting a "regular" (non-machine) recipe to one you can try in your machine. It may tale one or two trials to perfect the recipe, but the chances are good that you can successfully make the conversion. Before converting a recipe, make sure that it is a yeast bread recipe. As mentioned above, most bread machines are not designed to handle batter breads using chemically based leavenings such as baking powder and baking soda.

BASIC STEPS

The four basic steps to convert a recipe are:

1. Cut the recipe down so it will make one loaf. Many recipes are designed to make two loaves and you will need to cut these in half because you will need a single-loaf recipe.
2. Determine the parameters of your particular bread machine.
3. Determine the liquidity ratio of the recipe. This is the "stiffness" of the dough. This is important because your machine has a rather narrow range of doughs it can handle.
4. Determine the overall bulk of the recipe. You do not want a recipe that is too large for your machine.

Let's look at each of these steps in turn, with particular attention to the details involved in each step. Once you have accomplished a few conversions, you will no longer need to refer to this book because the steps are not really so complex as they might seem at first.

Step One:
REDUCE THE RECIPE SIZE

Most recipes will tell you how many loaves they make. Some will even tell you the approximate size of each loaf. Cut the recipe down so it will make one loaf. This may involve some calculations on your part, so a good techniquc is to write down the new recipe as you deduce it from the original.

If the recipe doesn't say how many loaves it makes, you can make a rough judgement by looking at the amount of flour required. A 1-pound loaf of bread will require about two cups of flour. Thus, if your recipe calls for six cups of all-purpose flour, you can probably figure that it will make three 1-pound loaves, or two 1$^{1}/_{2}$-pound loaves, or three 2-pound loaves.

Step Two:
DETERMINE THE PARAMETERS OF YOUR MACHINE

Since each machine varies in its capacity and motor power, you must determine the acceptable ranges for your machine in two categories: liquidity ratio and bulk. Table 2 shows the acceptable liquidity ratio ranges. To find you machine's range, look at the basic white bread recipe that came with the machine. Determine the number of cups of flour called for, and follow that column until you find the row that shows the number of ounces of liquid (water or milk) called for in the recipe. In that box you will find the ratio range for your machine. Highlight or write down that ratio range (see page 124, where you can write down information about your bread machine.)

Bulk is also simply calculated by determining the number of cups of flour called for in the basic white bread recipe for your machine. If the recipe calls for 2 to 2½ cups of flour, you have a 1-pound machine. If the recipe calls for 3 to 4 cups of flour, you have a 1½ pound (or greater) machine.

Once you have written this information down, you will, in the future, be able to skip this step and move right from step one to step three.

Table 2:
BREAD MACHINE LIQUIDITY RATIOS

Ounces Liquid	CUPS OF FLOUR: 2 Cups	2½ Cups	3 Cups	3½ Cups
5	2.9–3.3	3.6–4.4	4.3–5.3	5.0–6.2
6	**2.4–3.0**	3.0–3.6	3.6–4.4	4.2–5.2
7	**2.1–2.5**	2.6–3.2	3.1–3.7	3.6–4.4
8	1.8–2.2	2.3–2.8	2.7–3.3	3.2–3.9
9	1.6–2.0	2.0–2.4	**2.4–3.0**	2.8–3.4
10	1.4–1.8	1.8–2.2	**2.2–2.6**	2.5–3.1
11	1.4–1.7	1.6–2.0	2.0–2.4	2.3–2.8

Notes: (1 Cup) = 8 ounces. Bold entries show the most common bread machine ratio ranges. The ratio is computed by dividing dry ingredients by liquid ingredients. Higher ratios indicate stiffer dough; lower ratios indicate more liquid dough.

Step Three:
DETERMINE THE LIQUIDITY RATIO

Now you must determine the liquidity ratio (dough stiffness) of the recipe you are trying to convert. Table 3 (page 24) is a handy chart that you can duplicate and use each time you convert a recipe. To use the chart, simply fill in the ingredients and the amount called for in the original recipe. Write the amount in decimals (so your calculator can add them later) in the appropriate column. For example, if the recipe calls for 21/ 2 cups of flour, enter 2.5 in the DRY Cup column. You will have to make a judgement as to whether the ingredient is dry or wet. In general, use the form that the ingredient is in when you add it. An exception to this would be an ingredient that is going to melt when heat is applied. They are considered liquids. Typical ingredients in this category would include butter, margarine, fresh cheeses, and shortening.

Some ingredients should not be computed. Do not include the following ingredients in the calculation:

1. Yeast
2. Raisins or nuts added at the mix cycle
3. Seeds added at the mix cycle

You should count raisins, nuts, and seeds added initially as dry ingredients. The general rule is that if the ingredient will add to the stiffness of the dough, count it as a dry ingredient.

After you have entered all the ingredients, total each column and place the sum in the subtotal box. Then multiply each subtotal by the multiplier specified and place the result in the total box. Add the totals for dry ingredients together for a grand total (in teaspoons) and do the same for wet ingredients. Finally, divide the dry grand total by the wet grand total to compute the ratio for this recipe.

For best results, the ratio should fall within the liquidity ratio range designation for your machine (see Step Two). If it only misses by a few points, it will probably be satisfactory. If the ratio for the recipe is below the range, your dough might be too wet. Try a slight reduction in liquid ingredients or an increase in dry ingredients and recalculate. If the ratio is above the range, it is too dry. Either reduce the dry ingredients slightly, or add liquid.

Chances are, you will still need to experiment to get the recipe just right, but this calculation will give you a good start and place you well beyond the "trial and error" stage.

Step Four:
DETERMINE THE OVERALL BULK
You certainly do not want to overflow your machine with your test recipe, so make sure the bulk does not exceed the capacity of your machine. If you have a 1 pound machine, you should make sure your recipe does not call for more that 2½ cups of flour. If you have a 1½ pound machine, 3½ to 3¾ cups of flour are about the limit. For a 2 pound machine, 4 to 5 cups would be the limit. If you need to adjust the recipe, make sure you make equal adjustments of wet and dry ingredients to maintain the liquidity ratio of the recipe.

IMPROVING & TAILORING YOUR RECIPES

After your initial attempt at your newly converted recipe, you may want to adjust the recipe to increase or decrease bulk, reduce or increase rise, or alter texture or taste. Experiment with the recipe until you have perfected it. Part of the enjoyment of a bread machine is being able to try new and exciting recipes and to be creative. Although the conversion process, as presented here, may seem somewhat better suited to a mathematician than an artist, science and art go hand in hand in bread baking. Once you get to know your machine and your ingredients, you will feel comfortable making substitutions, or even trying brand new creations, made from scratch.

Table 3:
DOUGH LIQUIDITY CALCULATION WORKSHEET

	DRY			WET			
Ingredient	**t**	**T**	**C**	**t**	**T**	**C**	**oz**
Subtotal							
Multiplier		**3**	**48**		**3**	**48**	**6**
Total							
Grand Total							
Liquidity Ratio							

Instructions: 1. Use decimals for fractions (.5 teaspoon, etc.) 2. Subtotal each column. 3. Multiply the subtotal by the multiplier to obtain the total. 4. Add the dry totals and the wet totals separately to obtain the wet and dry grand totals. 5. Divide the dry grand total by the wet grand total to get the liquidity ratio.

RECIPE POINTERS

RECIPE SIZES

Three sizes are given for each of the recipes in this book, although smaller, and some larger, sizes are possible. I found in experimenting with a possible 3/4 pound size loaf that the machines tended to overbake the small loaves, and that they typically were too dry. Consequently, I decided to present here only the three sizes that will be accommodated by virtually all bread machines.

Recipe sizes refer to finished weight, not dimensions. The finished dimensions of the bread will depend to a great extent on baking conditions, amounts of yeast used, and types of ingredients. A 1-pound loaf of white bread, for example, might be larger than a 1 1/2-pound loaf of rye bread, which tends to be more densely textured.

MODIFICATIONS FOR SPECIFIC MACHINES

I have tried to include recipes that will work in any machine. On the 1-pound recipes, I found virtually no difference when testing the recipes in different machines. With the larger loaves, however, I noticed that some machines will no tolerate a stiff dough as well as others. If your machine's motor seems to be laboring with a certain dough, you might consider adding an extra tablespoon or two tablespoons more liquid. This will lower the liquidity ratio slightly, making the dough less stiff. As mentioned previously, you will come to recognize the "normal" sounds of your machine and will be able to identify those situations when slight recipe modifications are needed.

The other major difference between machines is in their rise cycles and the amount of yeast called for. I have tried to optimize the amount of yeast in the recipes to be suitable to all machines. If your machine has a dispenser or other device that causes a change in the amount of yeast normally used, you should make the modification to the amount of yeast in the recipe.

Many machines have "rapid bread" cycles that allow you to bake a loaf faster (single rise, rather than the usual double rise). When using the rapid bread cycle on your machine, double the amount of yeast that is normally called for, or consult your owner's manual for the proper yeast adjustment.

INGREDIENTS

There is a wide variety of ingredients called for in these recipes. Many are available at your local supermarket, but some must be purchased at health food stores. Some mail order sources are available if you do not have a health food store nearby. Here is a summary of important information about some of the main ingredients used in the recipes in this book.

WHITE FLOURS

All wheat-based flours are made from various combinations of three different varieties of wheat: hard wheat, soft wheat, and durum wheat. Of the three, hard wheat is highest in protein content and best for breadmaking. Soft wheat makes finer flour with less protein content. Durum wheat is used for semolina flour, which is a high-protein flour specifically used for pasta making. Flours vary by the combination of these wheat types used.

There are two main types of white flours, *all-purpose flour* and *bread flour.* All-purpose flour is made from from about 80% hard wheat and 20% soft wheat. Bread flour is made from 100% hard wheat, giving it slightly better breadmaking characteristics. Both varieties are available in most grocery stores. Bread flour is slightly higher in gluten content than all-purpose flour and will usually rise more. You should try to use the type of flour called for in the recipe. Substituting all-purpose flour for bread flour is permissible; however, it may slightly change the texture of the bread and cause it to rise less.

You will also note that all-purpose flour is available both in *bleached* and *unbleached* varieties. Bleached flour is treated during the milling process with chlorine, which shortens the processing time in whitening the flour. Unbleached flour is refined without the chlorination, but takes longer to process as a result, and will generally cost more. If the process has been speeded up by the addition of a chemical called bromate, the flour will be labeled as "bromated" flour.

On supermarket shelves you will often see pastry flour, cake flour, and self-rising flours. Pastry flour and cake flour are very finely ground flours and are made from 100% soft wheat. They are not suitable for breadmaking. Self-rising flour contains salt and baking soda and is not useful for breadmaking either.

WHOLE GRAINS

Whole Wheat Flour: This flour is ground from the complete wheat berry and contains the wheat germ and the wheat bran. It is coaser and heavier than white flour, and does not rise much. I purchase fresh wheat in bulk and grind it myself for the best-tasting bread; however, this may be more than most people can do. Grocery stores carry whole wheat flour, usually right alongside the white flour.

Graham Flour: In the early 20th century, Sylvester Graham publicly argued the merits of grains in the diet, wheat in particular. Graham flour is essentially equivalent to whole wheat flour, except that the milling process varies somewhat, with a slightly coarser grind and larger particles of bran throughout. This gives it a sweeter flavor than whole wheat flour. In recipes calling for graham flour, you may freely substitute whole wheat flour if graham flour is not available.

Semolina Flour: This is whole grain durum wheat with the bran layer removed. It can be used for breadmaking, particularly when used in combination with bread flour.

Bran: Bran is the outer covering of the kernel of wheat or oat. It is rich in fibre and is called for in small quantities in some recipes. Recently, much has been said about the benefits of oat bran. Both oat and wheat bran are available at most grocery stores.

Wheat Germ: This part of the wheat grain is readily available in grocery stores. Like bran, it is used sparingly in recipes. Wheat germ should be kept in the refrigerator after the container is opened.

Gluten Flour: Gluten is a protein found in the wheat berry. Gluten is necessary for rising to occur. When mixed with water, it forms an elastic substance that catches the gas bubbles formed by the leavening agent. Flours made from wheat, including whole wheat flour, white flour, and bread flour, contain plenty of gluten, but some whole grain flours do not. I have found that some gluten flour added to the mix when using a low-gluten flour will make for better rising and texture. Gluten flour can be purchased at any good health food store. A few recipes call for gluten flour, but most make it optional. Some people are allergic to gluten. Those individuals should stick to low-gluten flours, including rye and quinoa.

Rye Flour: This flour is very low in gluten content, so it will not rise when used by itself. Most of the recipes in this book call for a mixture of rye and another flour with a higher gluten content. This will let the bread rise.

Barley Flour: Barley flour lends a sweet taste and smooth texture to bread. Most recipes call for it in combination with white or wheat flour, since it has no gluten content. You will probably have to go to a health food store to find barley flour.

Buckwheat: Buckwheat is a strong-tasting flour for which some aficionados have acquired a real taste. In spite of its name, it is not made from wheat. Buckwheat is actually a grass, which yields groats, which can then be ground into flour. It is usually used in somewhat small quantities, but if you develop a liking for the strong flavor it presents, you can use it in combination with whole wheat flour. Called *kasha* in some parts of the world.

Cracked Wheat: As its name implies, this is part of the wheat berry. It is very hard and usually requires some soaking before use. It is widely available at health food stores and can often also be found in grocery stores.

7-Grain Cereal: This cereal has an appearance similar to cracked wheat, but consists of seven grains, including wheat, barley, corn, and oats. It is available at health food stores.

Oats: Use rolled oats (oatmeal) for your oat recipes. Just use the type available at the grocery store. When measuring rolled oats, pack them down into the measuring cup to get a full measure.

Oat Flour: This is flour ground specifically for bread from the oat groats. Since it has no gluten content, it has to be used in combination with a wheat flour of some kind.

Quinoa: This flour is imported from South America; it was a staple grain of the Incas in ancient times. It has one of the highest protein contents of any grain, and gives bread a somewhat nutty flavor.

Soy Flour: This flour is ground from soybeans; it is high in protein content at about 40—50%. It is very nutritious, but not flavorful, and is often used as an ingredient for enriching the nutritional value of bread.

Millet: This is a small, yellow, perfectly round grain. It can be used in bread whole, raw or cooked, or milled into flour.

Rice: Rice, a staple throughout the world, can be cooked and added to bread, or made into flour. The flour absorbs moisture more slowly than most flours, so it is well known among bakers as an excellent flour for dusting breads and pizza.

LIQUIDS

Water: Water is called for in most recipes. It should be used warm (between 100 and 110°F (37.8 to 43.3°C). I have found that hot tap water works fine. Don't heat the water any further, because water that is too hot can kill the yeast.

Milk: When milk is called for in a recipe, I use 1% or skim milk. In fact, the nutritional counts in the recipes in this book are calculated using values for 1% milk. If you do not have milk on hand, try using dry milk and adding the requisite amount of water to the recipe. Milk should usually be warmed to 100 to 110°F (37.8 to 43.3°C); the microwave works well for this at 45 seconds on high. Be careful not to overheat the milk, or you will kill the yeast.

Buttermilk: You can use buttermilk in its fresh form, or purchase buttermilk powder to mix it as needed. I do the latter, since I don't particularly like to drink buttermilk, and since recipes usually call for only small amounts. In most recipes, it is safe to substitute low-fat or skim milk for buttermilk. You may sacrifice some flavor, but it will result in a lower fat content for your bread.

Cream: There are several types of cream available at most grocery stores: heavy cream, light cream, whipping cream, and half-and-half. Some recipes call for heavy or light cream, but I have found that whipping cream works fine in most cases where cream is called for. Note that *whipping cream* and *whipped cream* are different. Whipped cream has had sugar added and is already in whipped form. Whipping cream comes in a carton and pours like milk.

Eggs: Most of the recipes in this book have been formulated to call for whole eggs, rather than portions of eggs or egg whites only. However, if you are concerned about the cholesterol in eggs, you may freely substitute any commercially available egg substitute. Use 1/4 cup (4 tablespoons) of egg substitute instead of each whole egg. You also may use powdered eggs, 1/4 cup of mixed eggs instead of each whole egg.

Butter: Many of the recipes in this book call for butter. You may substitute margarine or vegetable oil in the same quantities for butter. Butter, however, will provide the most flavor. I keep my butter in the freezer because spoilage is the biggest problem with real butter. When I need butter, I remove it from the freezer, cut the required quantity from the cube, and replace the butter in the freezer. It takes only a few minutes for the portion of butter to get to room temperature; then it can be placed in the bread pan. There is no need to melt butter or margarine before adding to the recipes, but it is best if the butter chunks are 1 tablespoon or smaller.

Olive Oil: I have used olive oil exclusively in these recipes, instead of calling for other oils. The taste is better and olive oil has no cholesterol. However, if you prefer another type of cooking oil, such as canola, corn oil, or any other vegetable oil, you may freely substitute. If you use olive oil, use a good grade of extra virgin olive oil.

OTHER INGREDIENTS

Salt: Salt is a yeast inhibitor, and is necessary in most recipes. If you are on a salt-restricted diet, you can eliminate the salt from the recipes. You should know, however, that if you do so, the characteristics of the bread will change. The bread will rise differently; it may rise too much and then collapse. The resulting texture may also be differernt. Keep in mind that other ingredients often have salt content. If you are on a salt-restricted diet, check the nutritional values for each recipe to see if there are "hidden salts" in the recipe. Butter, for example, is one of the ingredients that has a sodium content. Avoid using salt substitute as alternatives. They are chemically based and do not have the yeast inhibiting properties of real salt. They will do no good, and they may cause other chemical reactions that will change the properties of your bread.

Yeast: The recipes in this book call for yeast in teaspoons. I use active dry yeast, and I buy it in bulk. If kept in the refrigerator, it will last a long time. In fact, with my bread machine running, a supply of yeast doesn't last long at all. If you use cake yeast, you will need to make the conversion from teaspoons. If you purchase yeast in packets at the grocery store, one packet contains one scant tablespoon, or about 2¼ teaspoons of yeast. Do not use rapid rise yeast in these recipes.

Not all bread machines use the same amount of yeast in the large recipes. This is due to differences in cycle lengths and the yeast dispensing mechanisms available on a few machines. If a recipe does not rise enough, try adding an extra ½ teaspoon of yeast.

Yeast feeds on sugars and is inhibited by salts. It likes a warm environment, but too much heat will kill it. Most traditional bread recipes will require you to "proof" your yeast before using it. Proofing means mixing the yeast with sugar and warm (105 to 110°F, 40.6 to 43.3°C) water to allow it to become active before adding it to the recipe. Proofing is not necessary with bread machines; however, it is a good technique to use if you want to make sure your yeast is active (not too old). Yeast can be placed directly into the bread pan. When it touches liquid, it will begin to be active.

Sugars and Sweeteners: These are necessary in all bread recipes because they provide food for the yeast. Recipes in this book call for sugar (white, granulated), honey, syrup, molasses, or brown sugar. Molasses comes in various types, but I use blackstrap when baking. I have tried others, and haven't noticed any appreciable difference in the outcome, so use whatever molasses you happen to have on hand if a recipe calls for it. By the way, if the recipe calls for olive oil and honey or molasses, measure the olive oil first and don't rinse the spoon off. The honey or molasses will slide right out of the spoon into your pan!

Dough Enhancer: This product is difficult to find. Even health food stores may not carry it. You can find it at baking specialty stores or obtain it through mail order. Dough enhancer is a tofu (soybean) based powder that makes the dough smoother, and it is what commercial bakers often use to obtain the smooth-textured bread you buy at the store.

Spices, Nuts, and Seeds: These ingredients are called for in wide variety in recipes. I found most of the spices, seeds, and nuts called for in these recipes at the grocery store. If you cannot find them, you might try your health food store, which will usually stock some of the lesser known spices. Feel free to experiment with spices, adding more of spices you like and deleting those you do not. Often it is the blend of spices that makes the flavor, rather than any single spice, in those recipes calling for two or three different spices.

You will find that your spice cabinet enlarges as you bake more breads. Eventually, you will have a stock of almost any spice called for in a recipe. Preserving spices and seeds is not a problem, but preserving fresh nuts is. A few recipes call for fresh-chopped nuts. Use any type of nuts you enjoy, but keep in mind that nuts will go rancid if not used in a short period, so keep your supply of nuts fresh.

THE ORDER OF INGREDIENTS

There are two ways to place ingredients in the baking pan: Dry ingredients first or wet ingredients first. Most machines call for wet ingredients first, so that order is used in this book. Actually, dry first will work in all machines, except when you want to use a timed bake function. In that case, you will not want to activate the yeast until the baking process starts, so wet ingredients will have to go first, with yeast last. The machines that recommend dry ingredients first call for yeast as the first ingredient, followed by the other dry ingredients and, finally, the liquids. If your machine calls for dry ingedients first, add the ingredients to the pan in reverse order from that listed here.

PREPARATION OF INGREDIENTS

Most bread recipes call for all ingredients to be at room temperature, except for liquids, which are sometimes called for at 105 to 110°F (40.6 to 43.3°C). I have experimented with this and have not had real problems adding refrigerated ingredients. Rather than worry too much, just try setting all of your ingredients out first and then adding them. Once you get to the refrigerated ingredients, they have usually approached room temperature anyway.

When warm water is called for, it should be in the 105 to 110°F (40.6 to 43.3°C) range. I used to use a thermometer to make sure that the water was the correct temperature; however, I soon gave up on that when I found that hot tap water usually approached that range. Hot tap water varies, however, so make sure that yours is not too hot (too hot presents a much bigger problem than too cold).

Milk can be measured and then left to reach room temperature, or you can use the microwave to warm it up. Just be sure that if you use the microwave, you don't overheat the milk, which is easy to do in the microwave. If you overheat it, let it sit until it cools to 110°F (43.3°C) or lower before adding it to the bread pan.

For measuring flour and dry ingedients, I use the dip-and-level method, rather than the spoon method. For the dip-and-level method, simply dip your measuring cup into the flour and level it with a knife or other flat edge.

MAKING SUBSTITUTIONS AND MODIFICATIONS

I would recommend that you try the recipes as given the first time. Then if you want to make substitutions or modifications, experiment all you want. I have found that the best way to experiment is to alter one item at a time. If you alter too many things at once and the recipe fails, you will not be able to determine the cause of the failure. However, if you only altered one ingredient, you will know that the alteration was the only variable that could have caused failure.

You can freely make the substitutions mentioned in the ingredients section, including margarine for butter, low-fat or skim milk for buttermilk, egg substitutes for whole eggs, and all-purpose flour for bread flour. Keep in mind, however, that these substitutions will alter the original recipe somewhat and results will be different.

Avoid the use of chemically based substitutes, such as sugar and salt substitutes. These chemically based products may taste the same in coffee or soft drinks, but they break down differently from sodium or sugar in baking environments and will not work properly with yeast breads. It is better simply to eliminate salt, for example, than to use a salt substitute. Yeast feeds fine on sugar, but doesn't have much of a taste for artificial sweeteners.

Once you have gained a feel for a recipe, and for your machine, feel free to experiment. Most of the recipes in this book were developed that way, and you can have a lot of fun trying new and wonderful ideas. It is best to begin with established recipes and make successive alterations until you arrive at the perfect bread. Be sure and keep a log of your changes and the results. That way you can learn as you go and won't repeat mistakes. It also helps to have a basic understanding of the principles of baking with yeast, and of the characteristics of the ingredients you are using.

SLICING YOUR BREAD

When you get that loaf out of the machine, it smells wonderful. In fact, it has probably filled the whole house with the unmistakable odor of baking bread! You may want to dig in and eat the whole loaf right on the spot. Of course, you can do that. There is nothing better than fresh, hot bread. However, if your aim is to slice the bread and keep it for a few days, or use it for tomorrow's breakfast or lunch, then you will need to slice it more carefully.

Bread is best sliced after it has had a chance to cool completely. It then regains some of its stiffness and is much easier to handle. Slicing hot bread is a bit like trying to slice jello. As you cut, the bread gives, and it is difficult to get a good, straight slice.

For best results, remove your bread from the machine as soon as the "all done" alarm sounds. Place it on a cooling rack and let it cool completely (probably an hour or so). Although many machines now include cooling cycles, they cannot completely cool the bread, because the bread is still in the pan, where moisture and heat are trapped.

To slice the bread, use a serrated knife designed especially for slicing bread. Use a sawing motion and let the knife do the work. Putting too much downward pressure on the bread will smash it down and will give you uneven slices.

I inherited a meat slicer and don't use it for meat at all, but I have found it to be a wonderful bread slicer. I just set the thickness and the serrated blade cuts right through my cool loaf. If you have a slicer and your loaf is too big for it (the Welbilt loaves are too big for mine), cut the loaf in half lengthwise, making two half rounds. Then slice each half loaf with your slicer.

NUTRITIONAL VALUES

I am convinced that much of the consumer motivation behind the boom in bread machines sales is due to a desire to eat healthier foods. Whole grain breads are wonderful sources of nutrients, have no chemical preservatives, and taste great.

Each recipe is followed by the nutritional values. The values are per loaf, so to obtain a serving value, estimate how many slices you will make from the loaf and divide the value by the number of slices in the loaf. The nutritional values are estimates only, and should not be construed as anything else. They were derived by using *MasterCook* software package. Each of the ingredients in the recipes was calculated and totaled for each size of loaf. Below is an explanation of some of the main values used.

Calories are total calories for a loaf.

Protein is measured in grams. You will not find breads to be high in protein content, but when taken with other foods (Meats or legumes like beans) that are high in protein, a healthy combination is made.

Carbohydrates are also measured in grams. Carbohydrates, especially from whole grain sources, provide a good ratio of nutrients to calories (the opposite of "empty calories") and should constitute 45 to 48% of our daily intake of calories.

Fat is listed as total fat and saturated fat. We should try to reduce the amount of fats in our diet, and saturated fats should be avoided as much as possible. Government recommendations are that we limit our total calories from fat to 30% of our daily intake of calories, and limit saturated fat calories to only 10%. I have computed the percentage of calories from fat for each recipe, in addition to giving you the amount of total fat and saturated fat in grams. These breads are very healthy from the standpoint of percentage of calories from fats.

Cholesterol content is measured in milligrams. Cholesterol is only found in animal fats.

Sodium is measured for each recipe (in milligrams); it can derive not only from the salt added to the recipe, but from the sodium content of some other recipe ingredients. If you are on a low-sodium diet, you can reduce the salt content of the loaf, with the limitations discussed previously.

Fiber is important to a growing number of health-conscious individuals. The fiber content of each recipe is measured in grams. Fiber takes several forms, and so the figure given is a total figure that includes both dietary and crude fiber. Most nutritionists would recommend at least 25 grams of fiber per day in your diet.

RECIPE TESTING

Your strategy for testing recipes should be to try the 1-pound loaf first, even if you have a 1½ or 2 pound capacity machine. This offers three advantages:

1. You can make sure you like the taste and texture of the bread, while using a small quantity of ingredients for the first test.
2. You can make sure the bread works well in your machine with fewer ingredients at risk.
3. You can make sure that your particular baking conditions will not produce an oversize loaf, with little risk of a mess if they do.

Once you have tested a bread, make alterations to suit your taste, baking conditions, and machine. For example, you can increase or reduce yeast amounts, liquidity, substitute seeds or nuts, or make other ingredient substitutions. I would highly recommend, however, that you try the recipe once as given before making your own modifications. That gives you a basis upon which to make your changes and a point of reference, as discussed earlier. After that, be creative.

THE HISTORY OF BREAD

It is unclear where the wheat plant originated. Historians know that it was cultivated in southwestern Asia as early as 15,000 BC. In 1948, archeologists from the University of Chicago unearthed an Iraqi village, dated at about 6,700 BC, and found the berries from several types of wheat.

Over the centuries, it probably became obvious to early people, mostly nomadic hunters and gatherers, that the wheat plant could be cultivated. These early farmers also discovered that wheat could be stored and used as both food and seed for the next crop.

Early man probably chewed wheat berries, rather than grinding and baking them. Later, he learned to grind the wheat into flour and use it to make an early form of hot cereal or porridge. Eventually, he learned to bake the dough. This early bread was not leavened, and was probably a densely textured flat bread.

Around 3,000 BC, the Egyptians discovered how to make leavened bread. As leavening was developed, originally with the use of sourdough starters, wheat remained the grain of choice, since it had the best properties and cellular structure for rising. Egyptian traders spread the idea to Greece and Rome, where hundreds of varieties of bread were developed.

In medieval Europe, baker's guilds were developed, as baking bread became both an occupation and an art form.

Commercial bread, as we know it, is a relatively recent product. As late as the 1940s, most bread eaten in America was homemade. Today, millions of loaves of bread are baked daily in completely automated bakeries, but the quality of the bread has been somewhat compromised in the process, due to the addition of preservatives to lengthen shelf life and other time-saving manufacturing devices.

Today, the best bread is still homemade. Bread machines were developed to give you the best of both worlds: convenience and homemade quality. You can choose the type of bread you want, control the ingredients, and eat it fresh from the oven (or bread machine).

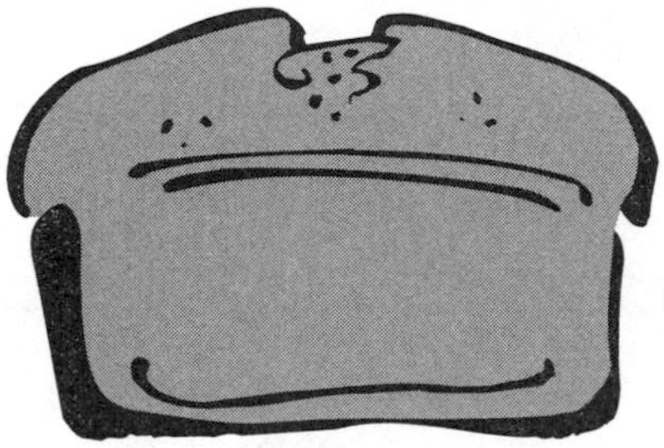

WHITE BREADS

The recipes in this section are all variations of white bread. They are typically finely textured and high rising, and they go well with just about any other food. The breads range from slightly sweet to spicy to fruity. Experiment with the recipes by substituting the fruits, nuts, and spices of your choice.

WHITE BREADS

Basic White Bread

The best white-bread recipe I have found for the bread machine. It is consistently good when baked in different machines and goes with about any meal. It also makes excellent toast.

INGREDIENTS

1 1/2-Pound Recipe		1-Pound Recipe
1 teaspoon	**active dry yeast**	1/2 teaspoon
3 tablespoons	**sugar**	2 tablespoons
3 cups	**bread flour**	2 cups
1 1/2 teaspoons	**salt**	1 teaspoon
1 1/2 tablespoons	**butter**	1 tablespoon
4 1/2 ounces	**warm milk**	3 ounces
4 1/2 ounces	**warm water**	3 ounces

NOTE:
For Panasonic/National machines, use 2 teaspoons of yeast for the 1 1/2-pound loaf.

NUTRITIONAL ANALYSIS

	1 1/2-Pound	1-Pound	
Total **Calories**	1837	1234	
Total **Protein**	55	36	grams
Total **Carbohydrates**	341	227	grams
Total **Fat**	26	17	grams
Total **Saturated Fat**	12	8	grams
Total **Cholesterol**	52	35	milligrams
Total **Sodium**	3276	2184	milligrams
Total **Fiber**	6	4	grams
% **Calories from Fat**	13	13	

Challah Bread (Jewish Egg Bread)

A festive white bread, challah is rich with eggs, butter, and honey. You will find it much richer than basic white bread.

INGREDIENTS

$1^1/_2$-Pound Recipe		1-Pound Recipe
$2^1/_2$ teaspoons	**active dry yeast**	$1^1/_2$ teaspoons
$1^1/_2$ teaspoons	**poppy seeds**	1 teaspoon
3 cups	**bread flour**	2 cups
$1^1/_2$ teaspoons	**salt**	1 teaspoon
3 tablespoons	**honey**	2 tablespoons
3 tablespoons	**butter**	2 tablespoons
3	**eggs**	2
6 ounces	**warm water**	4 ounces

NOTE:
For Panasonic/National machines, use $3^1/_2$ teaspoons of yeast for the $1^1/_2$ pound loaf.

NUTRITIONAL ANALYSIS

	$1^1/_2$-Pound	1-Pound	
Total **Calories**	2230	1486	
Total **Protein**	72	48	grams
Total **Carbohydrates**	351	234	grams
Total **Fat**	58	39	grams
Total **Saturated Fat**	27	18	grams
Total **Cholesterol**	732	488	milligrams
Total **Sodium**	3401	2267	milligrams
Total **Fiber**	7	5	grams
% **Calories from Fat**	24	24	

Zuni Bread

This Southwest Indian bread combines the high-rising texture of white bread with the crunchiness of corn bread. It is excellent with a good, hot Southwestern chili. Note that all-purpose flour is used instead of bread flour in this recipe.

INGREDIENTS

1½-Pound Recipe		1-Pound Recipe
1½ teaspoons	**active dry yeast**	1 teaspoon
2½ cups	**all-purpose flour**	1¾ cups
¾ cup	**yellow cornmeal**	½ cup
1 teaspoon	**salt**	½ teaspoon
1½ tablespoons	**molasses**	1 tablespoon
1½ tablespoons	**olive oil**	1 tablespoon
1 cup	**warm water**	5½ ounces

NOTES:

1. For Panasonic/National machines, use 2½ teaspoons of yeast for the 1½-pound recipe.
2. For DAK/Welbilt machines, add 1 extra teaspoon of warm water in the 1½-pound recipe only.

NUTRITIONAL ANALYSIS

	1½-Pound	1-Pound	
Total **Calories**	1848	1273	
Total **Protein**	50	35	grams
Total **Carbohydrates**	341	236	grams
Total **Fat**	29	20	grams
Total **Saturated Fat**	4	3	grams
Total **Cholesterol**	0	0	milligrams
Total **Sodium**	2194	1107	milligrams
Total **Fiber**	16	11	grams
% Calories from Fat	14	14	

Sheepherder's Bread

This is a favorite of many of my testers, especially those who like French breads. The recipe is simple but tasty, like those used by sheepherder in days of old. Time this bread to be done right before dinner; then tear it apart, rather than slice it, while still hot. Note that all-purpose flour is used to give it an authentic texture.

INGREDIENTS

1½-Pound Recipe		1-Pound Recipe
1½ teaspoons	**active dry yeast**	1 teaspoon
2 tablespoons	**sugar**	4 teaspoons
3 cups	**all-purpose flour**	2 cups
1 teaspoon	**salt**	¼ teaspoon
2½ tablespoons	**butter**	1½ tablespoons
1 cup	**warm water**	5½ ounces

NOTE:
For Panasonic/National machines, use 2 teaspoons of yeast for the 1½-pound loaf.

NUTRITIONAL ANALYSIS

	1½-Pound	1-Pound	
Total **Calories**	1838	1208	
Total **Protein**	51	34	grams
Total **Carbohydrates**	323	216	grams
Total **Fat**	36	22	grams
Total **Saturated Fat**	19	11	grams
Total **Cholesterol**	78	47	milligrams
Total **Sodium**	2142	1073	milligrams
Total **Fiber**	7	4	grams
% **Calories from Fat**	17	16	

Ham & Cheese Bread

Real cheese and pieces of ham make this a tangy, tasty bread. It is very moist and rich. It's literally a sandwich in a loaf of bread.

INGREDIENTS

1 1/2-Pound Recipe		1-Pound Recipe
2 teaspoons	**active dry yeast**	1 1/2 teaspoons
3 1/2 teaspoons	**sugar**	2 1/2 teaspoons
1/4 cup	**ham pieces (chopped)**	3 tablespoons
1/2 cup	**Swiss cheese (grated)**	1/4 cup
2 1/2 tablespoons	**minced onion (dehydrated)**	5 teaspoons
3/4 cup	**cheddar cheese (grated)**	1/2 cup
1 1/2 teaspoons	**paprika**	1 teaspoon
2 1/2 tablespoons	**Parmesan cheese (grated)**	5 teaspoons
1 teaspoon	**dry mustard**	1/2 teaspoon
1/2 teaspoon	**salt**	1/4 teaspoon
2 1/2 cups	**bread flour**	1 3/4 cups
2 1/2 tablespoons	**butter**	5 teaspoons
7 ounces	**warm milk**	4 1/2 ounces

NOTES:

1. For Panasonic/National machines, use 3 teaspoons of yeast for the 1 1/2pound loaf.
2. This bread has a high liquid content, so the top may fall during baking.
3. Use a light crust setting. The crust will be somewhat darker than usual, due to the fresh cheese in the recipe.

NUTRITIONAL ANALYSIS

	1 1/2-Pound	1-Pound	
Total **Calories**	2354	1585	
Total **Protein**	97	64	grams
Total **Carbohydrates**	290	202	grams
Total **Fat**	89	57	grams
Total **Saturated Fat**	52	33	grams
Total **Cholesterol**	237	150	milligrams
Total **Sodium**	2698	2142	milligrams
Total **Fiber**	7	5	grams
% **Calories from Fat**	34	33	

Sour Cream Bread

Somewhat tangy with poppy seeds, this bread doesn't rise as much as traditional white breads. However, it is excellent for cold-cuts sandwiches.

INGREDIENTS

1$^{1}/_{2}$-Pound Recipe		1-Pound Recipe
1 teaspoon	**active dry yeast**	$^{1}/_{2}$ teaspoon
2 tablespoons	**sugar**	4 teaspoons
3 cups	**bread flour**	2 cups
1 tablespoon	**poppy seeds**	2 teaspoons
1$^{1}/_{2}$ teaspoons	**salt**	1 teaspoon
1 cup	**sour cream**	$^{3}/_{4}$ cup
1$^{1}/_{2}$ ounces	**warm water**	1 tablespoon

NOTES:

1. For Panasonic/National machines, use 2 teaspoons of yeast for the 1$^{1}/_{2}$-pound loaf.
2. For DAK/Welbilt machines, use 2 ounces of warm water in the 1$^{1}/_{2}$-pound loaf.

NUTRITIONAL ANALYSIS

	1$^{1}/_{2}$-Pound	1-Pound	
Total **Calories**	2122	1454	
Total **Protein**	59	40	grams
Total **Carbohydrates**	335	224	grams
Total **Fat**	59	43	grams
Total **Saturated Fat**	31	23	grams
Total **Cholesterol**	102	77	milligrams
Total **Sodium**	3331	2231	milligrams
Total **Fiber**	7	5	grams
% **Calories from Fat**	25	27	

Sally Lunn Bread

The origins of the name of this bread are unclear, but it is a rich variation on the white-bread theme with egg and extra sugar. It makes a rich sandwich bread and is excellent for toast. Sally Lunn is a high riser.

INGREDIENTS

$1^1/_2$-Pound Recipe		1-Pound Recipe
1 teaspoon	**active dry yeast**	$^1/_2$ teaspoon
4 tablespoons	**sugar**	3 tablespoons
3 cups	**bread flour**	2 cups
1 teaspoon	**salt**	$^1/_2$ teaspoon
5 ounces	**warm milk**	$3^1/_2$ ounces
2	**eggs**	1
$5^1/_2$ tablespoons	**butter**	$3^1/_2$ tablespoons
$^1/_2$ cup	**warm water**	$1^1/_2$ ounces

NOTE:
For Panasonic/National machines, use 2 teaspoons of yeast for the $1\ ^1/_2$-pound loaf.

NUTRITIONAL ANALYSIS

	$1^1/_2$-Pound	1-Pound	
Total **Calories**	2440	1601	
Total **Protein**	68	43	grams
Total **Carbohydrates**	355	241	grams
Total **Fat**	81	51	grams
Total **Saturated Fat**	44	28	grams
Total **Cholesterol**	603	326	milligrams
Total **Sodium**	2348	1191	milligrams
Total **Fiber**	6	4	grams
% Calories from Fat	30	28	

Picnic Bread

Picnic bread is fun for cold-cuts sandwiches because it already contains relish! This bread has a sweet and spicy taste and slightly yellow color. It looks and tastes great.

INGREDIENTS

1 1/2-Pound Recipe		1-Pound Recipe
1 1/2 teaspoons	**active dry yeast**	1 teaspoon
2 tablespoons	**sugar**	1 1/2 tablespoons
3 cups	**bread flour**	2 cups
1 1/2 teaspoons	**salt**	1 teaspoon
1/4 cup	**sweet pickle relish (drained)**	2 tablespoons
1 1/2 tablespoons	**butter**	1 tablespoon
6 1/2 ounces	**warm milk**	1/2 cup
3 tablespoons	**warm water**	2 tablespoons

NOTE:
For Panasonic/National machines, use 2 1/2 teaspoons of yeast for the 1 1/2-pound loaf.

NUTRITIONAL ANALYSIS

	1 1/2-Pound	1-Pound	
Total **Calories**	1904	1259	
Total **Protein**	58	38	grams
Total **Carbohydrates**	353	234	grams
Total **Fat**	27	18	grams
Total **Saturated Fat**	13	9	grams
Total **Cholesterol**	55	36	milligrams
Total **Sodium**	3735	2414	milligrams
Total **Fiber**	7	4	grams
% **Calories from Fat**	13	13	

Buttermilk & Honey Bread

This traditional farm bread is a good white-bread staple, making it excellent for sandwiches or toast.

INGREDIENTS

1½-Pound Recipe		1-Pound Recipe
1 teaspoon	**active dry yeast**	½ teaspoon
3 cups	**bread flour**	2 cups
1½ teaspoons	**salt**	1 teaspoon
½ teaspoon	**sugar**	½ teaspoon
1½ tablespoons	**honey**	1 tablespoon
1 tablespoon	**butter**	1 tablespoon
¾ cup	**buttermilk**	3 ounces
3 ounces	**warm water**	3 ounces

NOTE:
For machines with yeast dispensers, use 2 teaspoons of yeast for the 1½-pound loaf.

NUTRITIONAL ANALYSIS

	1½-Pound	1-Pound	
Total **Calories**	1777	1205	
Total **Protein**	58	37	grams
Total **Carbohydrates**	336	223	grams
Total **Fat**	20	17	grams
Total **Saturated Fat**	9	8	grams
Total **Cholesterol**	47	39	milligrams
Total **Sodium**	3323	2196	milligrams
Total **Fiber**	6	4	grams
% **Calories from Fat**	10	12	

Buttermilk-Potato Bread

The potato and buttermilk make this a richer-than-normal white bread. It's excellent with soup.

INGREDIENTS

1 1/2-Pound Recipe		1-Pound Recipe
1 1/2 teaspoons	**active dry yeast**	1 teaspoon
3 cups	**bread flour**	2 cups
1 1/2 teaspoons	**salt**	1 teaspoon
1 tablespoon	**sugar**	2 teaspoons
3 tablespoons	**instant mashed-potato flakes or buds**	2 tablespoons
5 ounces	**warm water**	3 1/2 ounces
1 tablespoon	**butter**	1/2 tablespoon
1/2 cup	**buttermilk**	1/3 cup

NOTE:
For machines with yeast dispensers, use 3 teaspoons of yeast for the 1 1/2-pound loaf.

NUTRITIONAL ANALYSIS

	1 1/2-Pound	1-Pound	
Total **Calories**	1748	1183	
Total **Protein**	57	41	grams
Total **Carbohydrates**	325	221	grams
Total **Fat**	22	13	grams
Total **Saturated Fat**	9	5	grams
Total **Cholesterol**	41	28	milligrams
Total **Sodium**	3420	2325	milligrams
Total **Fiber**	7	4	grams
% **Calories from Fat**	11	10	

Herb-Cheddar Bread

The spices and cheese in this bread give it a wonderful tangy taste and moist texture. It is especially good with soup or salad.

INGREDIENTS

1 1/2-Pound Recipe		1-Pound Recipe
1 1/2 teaspoons	**active dry yeast**	1 teaspoon
3 cups	**bread flour**	2 cups +2 tablespoons
1 teaspoon	**tarragon**	1/2 teaspoon
1 1/2 teaspoons	**chervil**	1 teaspoon
1 1/2 teaspoons	**basil**	1 teaspoon
1 teaspoon	**salt**	1/2 teaspoon
1 1/2 teaspoons	**sugar**	1 teaspoon
1/2 cup	**cheddar cheese (grated)**	1/3 cup
1 1/2 tablespoons	**olive oil**	1 tablespoons
7 ounces	**warm water**	5 ounces

NOTES:

1. For machines with yeast dispensers, use 3 teaspoons of yeast for the 1 1/2-pound loaf.
2. The dough ball will be somewhat dry at first, but this will change as the cheese is heated and melts. For low-power motors, the motor may labor with the large recipe. If this happens, add 2 extra tablespoons of warm water.

NUTRITIONAL ANALYSIS

	1 1/2-Pound	1-Pound	
Total **Calories**	1925	1366	
Total **Protein**	65	46	grams
Total **Carbohydrates**	306	221	grams
Total **Fat**	46	31	grams
Total **Saturated Fat**	16	10	grams
Total **Cholesterol**	60	39	milligrams
Total **Sodium**	2490	1303	milligrams
Total **Fiber**	7	5	grams
% **Calories from Fat**	22	20	

Honey-Seed Bread

This bread features four popular seeds. Substitute other seeds, if you like.

INGREDIENTS

1 1/2-Pound Recipe		1-Pound Recipe
1 1/2 teaspoons	**active dry yeast**	1 teaspoon
3 cups	**bread flour**	2 cups
1/2 tablespoon	**sesame seeds**	1 teaspoon
1/2 tablespoon	**poppy seeds**	1 teaspoon
1/2 tablespoon	**fennel seeds**	1 teaspoon
1 tablespoon	**sunflower seeds**	2 teaspoons
1 1/2 teaspoons	**salt**	1 teaspoon
1/2 teaspoon	**sugar**	1/2 teaspoon
1 tablespoon	**honey**	1/2 tablespoon
1 tablespoon	**butter**	1/2 tablespoon
9 ounces	**warm milk**	3/4 cup

NOTES:

1. For machines with yeast dispensers, use 3 teaspoons of yeast for the 1 1/2-pound loaf.
2. For machines with low-power motors, add 2 tablespoons of warm milk to the 1 1/2-pound recipe
3. Seeds may be added at the mix cycle beep, if your machine is so equipped.

NUTRITIONAL ANALYSIS

	1 1/2-Pound	1-Pound	
Total **Calories**	1932	1295	
Total **Protein**	65	44	grams
Total **Carbohydrates**	338	225	grams
Total **Fat**	34	24	grams
Total **Saturated Fat**	11	6	grams
Total **Cholesterol**	42	23	milligrams
Total **Sodium**	3354	2236	milligrams
Total **Fiber**	8	5	grams
% **Calories from Fat**	16	16	

WHITE BREADS

Jalapeño Cheese Bread

For best results, use cheddar cheese that's made with jalapeño peppers. Such cheese is available in most supermarkets.

INGREDIENTS

1$^1/_2$-Pound Recipe		**1-Pound Recipe**
2 teaspoons	**active dry yeast**	1$^1/_2$ teaspoons
1$^1/_4$ cups	**cheddar/jalapeño cheese (grated)**	$^3/_4$ cup
$^1/_2$ teaspoon	**cilantro (coriander)**	$^1/_2$ teaspoon
3$^1/_2$ teaspoons	**sugar**	2$^1/_2$ teaspoons
$^1/_2$ teaspoon	**salt**	$^1/_4$ teaspoon
1 teaspoon	**dry mustard**	$^1/_2$ teaspoon
2$^1/_2$ tablespoons	**dried minced onion**	1$^1/_2$ tablespoons
2$^1/_2$ cups	**bread flour**	1$^2/_3$ cups
7 ounces	**warm milk**	4$^1/_2$ ounces
2$^1/_2$ tablespoons	**butter**	1$^1/_2$ tablespoons

NOTE:
For machines with yeast dispensers, use 4 teaspoons of yeast for the 1$^1/_2$-pound loaf.

NUTRITIONAL ANALYSIS

	1$^1/_2$-Pound	**1-Pound**	
Total **Calories**	2262	1453	
Total **Protein**	87	56	grams
Total **Carbohydrates**	287	191	grams
Total **Fat**	84	51	grams
Total **Saturated Fat**	50	30	grams
Total **Cholesterol**	235	141	milligrams
Total **Sodium**	2062	1669	milligrams
Total **Fiber**	6	4	grams
% **Calories from Fat**	34	32	

Nut Bread

Nut bread is excellent with all kinds of cheese.

INGREDIENTS

$1^1/_2$-Pound Recipe		1-Pound Recipe
$1^1/_2$ teaspoons	**active dry yeast**	1 teaspoon
$2^1/_4$ cup+ 2 tablespoons	**bread flour**	$1^1/_2$ cups + 2 tablespoons
$^1/_2$ cup	**chopped or ground nuts**	$^1/_3$ cup
$^1/_2$ cup	**brown sugar**	$^1/_3$ cup
$^1/_2$ cup	**warm milk**	$2^1/_2$ ounces
1	**egg**	1
$^1/_2$ teaspoon	**walnut or almond extract**	$^1/_2$ teaspoon
$^1/_2$ teaspoon	**vanilla extract**	$^1/_2$ teaspoon
$2^1/_2$ tablespoons	**butter**	$1^1/_2$ tablespoons
$^1/_4$ cup	**warm water**	$1^1/_2$ ounces
1 teaspoon	**salt**	$^1/_2$ teaspoon
$1^1/_2$ teaspoons	**cinnamon**	1 teaspoon

NOTES:

1. For machines with yeast dispensers, use 3 teaspoons of yeast for the $1^1/_2$-pound loaf.
2. Measure the nuts whole before chopping or grinding them.

NUTRITIONAL ANALYSIS

	$1^1/_2$-Pound	1-Pound	
Total **Calories**	2365	1602	
Total **Protein**	60	42	grams
Total **Carbohydrates**	362	244	grams
Total **Fat**	78	51	grams
Total **Saturated Fat**	24	15	grams
Total **Cholesterol**	296	263	milligrams
Total **Sodium**	172	133	milligrams
Total **Fiber**	8	6	grams
% **Calories from Fat**	29	29	

Olive Bread

This bread has the flavor of olives and it has small olive pieces throughout the loaf.

INGREDIENTS

1½-Pound Recipe		1-Pound Recipe
1 teaspoon	**active dry yeast**	½ teaspoon
5 tablespoons	**black olives (chopped)**	3½ tablespoons
3 cups + 1 tablespoon	**bread flour**	2 cups
1 teaspoon	**salt**	½ teaspoon
2 tablespoons	**sugar**	1½ tablespoons
2 tablespoons	**olive oil**	1 tablespoon
9 ounces	**warm water**	¾ cup

NOTE:
For machines with yeast dispensers, use 2 teaspoons of yeast for the 1½-pound loaf.

NUTRITIONAL ANALYSIS

	1½-Pound	1-Pound	
Total **Calories**	1897	1212	
Total **Protein**	52	34	grams
Total **Carbohydrates**	332	219	grams
Total **Fat**	38	21	grams
Total **Saturated Fat**	5	3	grams
Total **Cholesterol**	0	0	milligrams
Total **Sodium**	2513	1332	milligrams
Total **Fiber**	8	5	grams
% **Calories from Fat**	18	16	

Potato-Sesame Bread

The soft texture from the potato flakes combined with the nutty flavor of the sesame seeds make this an excellent breakfast bread.

INGREDIENTS

1 1/2-Pound Recipe		1-Pound Recipe
1 teaspoon	**active dry yeast**	1/2 teaspoon
2 3/4 cups	**bread flour**	1 3/4 cups + 2 tablespoons
1 teaspoon	**parsley flakes**	1/2 teaspoon
3 tablespoons	**sesame seeds**	2 tablespoons
1 teaspoon	**salt**	1/2 teaspoon
4 tablespoons	**instant-mashed-potato flakes or buds**	3 tablespoons
1/2 cup	**instant dry milk**	3 tablespoons
2 tablespoons	**sugar**	1 1/2 tablespoons
1/2 cup	**buttermilk**	2 1/2 ounces
2	**eggs**	1
2 tablespoons	**butter**	1 1/2 tablespoons
5 ounces	**warm water**	1 1/2 ounces

NOTE:
For machines with yeast dispensers, use 2 teaspoons of yeast for the 1 1/2-pound loaf.

NUTRITIONAL ANALYSIS

	1 1/2-Pound	1-Pound	
Total **Calories**	2171	1473	
Total **Protein**	78	51	grams
Total **Carbohydrates**	333	229	grams
Total **Fat**	57	38	grams
Total **Saturated Fat**	21	14	grams
Total **Cholesterol**	503	269	milligrams
Total **Sodium**	2652	1414	milligrams
Total **Fiber**	7	5	grams
% Calories from Fat	24	23	

Raisin-Walnut Bread

This white bread has whole-grain flavor. If you like it sweeter, try doubling the sugar in the recipe.

INGREDIENTS

1 1/2-Pound Recipe		1-Pound Recipe
2 teaspoons	**active dry yeast**	1 1/2 teaspoons
2 1/4 cups	**bread flour**	1 1/2 cups
1/4 cup	**walnuts (chopped)**	2 tablespoons
1/4 cup	**golden raisins**	2 tablespoons
1/3 cup	**whole-wheat flour**	1/4 cup
2 tablespoons	**oat bran**	1 1/2 tablespoons
1/3 cup	**rye flour**	1/4 cup
1 teaspoon	**salt**	1/2 teaspoon
1 1/2 teaspoon	**sugar**	1 teaspoon
1/2 teaspoon	**walnut extract**	1/4 teaspoon
1 cup	**warm water**	6 1/2 ounces

NOTE:
For machines with yeast dispensers, use 3 1/2 teaspoons of yeast for the 1 1/2-pound loaf.

NUTRITIONAL ANALYSIS

	1 1/2-Pound	1-Pound	
Total **Calories**	1740	1137	
Total **Protein**	55	37	grams
Total **Carbohydrates**	327	218	grams
Total **Fat**	26	15	grams
Total **Saturated Fat**	3	2	grams
Total **Cholesterol**	0	0	milligrams
Total **Sodium**	2148	1076	milligrams
Total **Fiber**	20	14	grams
% **Calories from Fat**	14	12	

Shredded Wheat-Nut Bread

The small amount of shredded wheat cereal in this bread gives it a light but distinct wheat flavor, although it retains the texture and appearance of white bread.

INGREDIENTS

$1^1/_2$-Pound Recipe		1-Pound Recipe
1 teaspoon	**active dry yeast**	$^1/_2$ teaspoon
3 cups	**bread flour**	2 cups
$^1/_4$ cup	**chopped nuts**	3 tablespoons
1	**shredded wheat biscuit**	$^2/_3$
$^1/_2$ teaspoon	**salt**	$^1/_4$ teaspoon
1 teaspoon	**dry mustard**	$^1/_2$ teaspoon
1 tablespoon	**molasses**	$^1/_2$ tablespoon
$^1/_2$ tablespoon	**olive oil**	$^1/_2$ tablespoon
$^3/_4$ cup	**warm milk**	$^1/_2$ cup
$^1/_4$ cup	**warm water**	$1^1/_2$ ounces

NOTE:
For machines with yeast dispensers, use 2 teaspoons of yeast for the $1^1/_2$-pound loaf.

NUTRITIONAL ANALYSIS

	$1^1/_2$-Pound	1-Pound	
Total **Calories**	1939	1323	
Total **Protein**	62	42	grams
Total **Carbohydrates**	340	226	grams
Total **Fat**	35	27	grams
Total **Saturated Fat**	5	4	grams
Total **Cholesterol**	8	5	milligrams
Total **Sodium**	1184	609	milligrams
Total **Fiber**	8	5	grams
% Calories from Fat	16	18	

Sunflower Bread

This nutritious bread has the aroma and flavor of sunflower seeds. The sunflower-seed oil, released during baking, permeates the bread, giving it a distinctively nutty taste.

INGREDIENTS

1 1/2-Pound Recipe		1-Pound Recipe
1 1/2 teaspoons	**active dry yeast**	1 teaspoon
2 1/2 cups	**bread flour**	1 3/4 cups
4 tablespoons	**sunflower seeds**	2 1/2 tablespoons
1 1/ teaspoon	**salt**	1 teaspoon
1/2 cup	**oat bran**	1/3 cup
1 tablespoon	**sugar**	2 teaspoons
2 tablespoons	**molasses**	1 1/2 tablespoons
2 tablespoons	**butter**	1 tablespoon
1/2 cup	**warm milk**	3 ounces
4 1/2 ounces	**warm water**	1 1/2 ounces

NOTE:
For machines with yeast dispensers, use 3 teaspoons of yeast for the 1 1/2-pound loaf.

NUTRITIONAL ANALYSIS

	1 1/2-Pound	1-Pound	
Total **Calories**	1979	1310	
Total **Protein**	60	41	grams
Total **Carbohydrates**	327	224	grams
Total **Fat**	49	28	grams
Total **Saturated Fat**	18	10	grams
Total **Cholesterol**	67	35	milligrams
Total **Sodium**	3299	2207	milligrams
Total **Fiber**	12	8	grams
% **Calories from Fat**	22	20	

Walnut Bread

This bread has a great walnut flavor and crunch. It's excellent toasted with cheese.

INGREDIENTS

1$^{1}/_{2}$-Pound Recipe		1-Pound Recipe
2 teaspoons	**active dry yeast**	1$^{1}/_{2}$ teaspoons
2 cups	**bread flour**	1$^{1}/_{3}$ cups
$^{3}/_{4}$ cup	**walnuts (chopped)**	$^{1}/_{3}$ cup
1 teaspoon	**salt**	$^{1}/_{2}$ teaspoon
3 tablespoons	**brown sugar**	2 tablespoons
1 cup	**whole-wheat flour**	$^{2}/_{3}$ cup
$^{1}/_{2}$ teaspoon	**walnut extract**	$^{1}/_{4}$ teaspoon
5 ounces	**warm milk**	3 ounces
$^{1}/_{2}$ cup	**warm water**	3 ounces

NOTE:
For machines with yeast dispensers, use 3 teaspoons of yeast for the 1$^{1}/_{2}$-pound loaf.

NUTRITIONAL ANALYSIS

	1$^{1}/_{2}$-Pound	1-Pound	
Total **Calories**	2205	1467	
Total **Protein**	69	46	grams
Total **Carbohydrates**	351	234	grams
Total **Fat**	64	43	grams
Total **Saturated Fat**	7	5	grams
Total **Cholesterol**	6	4	milligrams
Total **Sodium**	2237	1131	milligrams
Total **Fiber**	24	16	grams
% **Calories from Fat**	26	26	

Walnut-Herb Bread

This bread has a spicy flavor in addition to the light walnut taste and crunch. You could substitute almonds, Brazil nuts, or pecans for walnuts.

INGREDIENTS

$1^1/_2$-Pound Recipe		1-Pound Recipe
$1^1/_2$ teaspoons	**active dry yeast**	1 teaspoon
3 cups	**bread flour**	2 cups
$^1/_4$ cup	**walnuts (chopped)**	2 tablespoons
$^1/_2$ teaspoon	**dill weed**	$^1/_4$ teaspoon
$^1/_2$ teaspoon	**oregano**	$^1/_4$ teaspoon
$^1/_2$ teaspoon	**dried parsley flakes**	$^1/_4$ teaspoon
$^1/_2$ teaspoon	**dried lemon peel**	$^1/_4$ teaspoon
$1^1/_2$ teaspoons	**salt**	1 teaspoon
1 tablespoon	**brown sugar**	2 teaspoons
$1^1/_2$ tablespoons	**butter**	1 tablespoon
9 ounces	**warm water**	$^3/_4$ cup

NOTES:

1. For machines with yeast dispensers, use 3 teaspoons of yeast for the $1^1/_2$-pound loaf.
2. If salted nuts are used, reduce the salt by $^1/_2$ teaspoon.

NUTRITIONAL ANALYSIS

	$1^1/_2$-Pound	1-Pound	
Total **Calories**	1893	1229	
Total **Protein**	55	36	grams
Total **Carbohydrates**	319	212	grams
Total **Fat**	43	25	grams
Total **Saturated Fat**	13	9	grams
Total **Cholesterol**	47	31	milligrams
Total **Sodium**	3215	2143	milligrams
Total **Fiber**	8	5	grams
% **Calories from Fat**	20	19	

Wheat Germ Bread

The addition of nutritious wheat germ gives this traditional white bread a slightly nutty flavor.

INGREDIENTS

1 1/2-Pound Recipe		1-Pound Recipe
1 1/2 teaspoons	**active dry yeast**	1 teaspoon
2 1/2 cups	**bread flour**	1 3/4 cups
1/2 cup	**wheat germ**	1/4 cup
2 teaspoons	**salt**	1 1/2 teaspoons
3 tablespoons	**olive oil**	2 tablespoons
2 tablespoons	**honey**	1 tablespoon
1 cup	**warm water**	5 ounces

NOTE:
For machines with yeast dispensers, use 3 teaspoons of yeast for the 1 1/2-pound loaf.

NUTRITIONAL ANALYSIS

	1 1/2-Pound	1-Pound	
Total **Calories**	2057	1275	
Total **Protein**	65	39	grams
Total **Carbohydrates**	340	207	grams
Total **Fat**	54	35	grams
Total **Saturated Fat**	7	5	grams
Total **Cholesterol**	0	0	milligrams
Total **Sodium**	4275	3205	milligrams
Total **Fiber**	13	7	grams
% **Calories from Fat**	24	25	

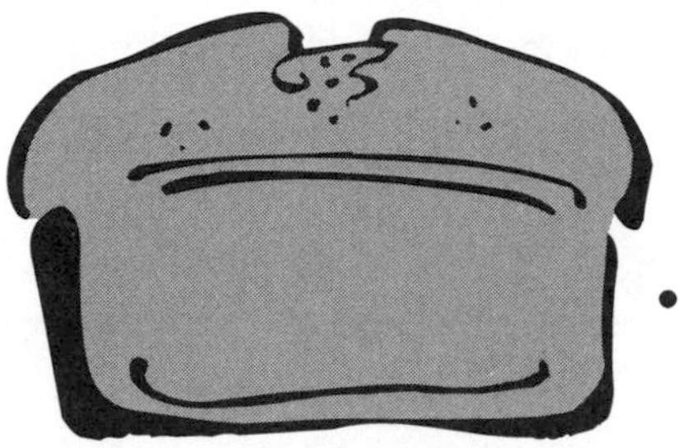

WHEAT BREADS

This section features breads that emphasize whole wheat, both in flavor and texture. The breads vary in the percentage of whole-wheat flour used, but each is unique in its distinctive wheat flavor combined with the flavors of other wonderful ingredients.

100% Wheat Bread

This recipe is one of the best I have tasted. It captures the essence of whole-grain bread with its rich wheat flavor and its somewhat crumbly texture. Spread honey on a toasted slice for an unbelievable taste treat.

INGREDIENTS

1 1/2-Pound Recipe		1-Pound Recipe
4 teaspoons	**active dry yeast**	2 1/2 teaspoons
3 tablespoons	**honey**	2 tablespoons
3 cups	**whole-wheat flour**	2 cups
2 teaspoons	**salt**	1 1/2 teaspoons
1/4 cup + 2 tablespoons	**wheat gluten**	1/4 cup
1 1/2 cups	**warm water**	1 cup

NOTES:

1. For Panasonic/National machines, use 4 teaspoons of yeast for the 1 1/2-pound loaf.
2. You will notice that the dough seems a little more liquid than usual. That is normal for this recipe, and the amount of liquid will yield a moist loaf. If the loaf collapses in your machine, cut back the liquid slightly (1 ounce or so) on the next try.

NUTRITIONAL ANALYSIS

	1 1/2-Pound	1-Pound	
Total **Calories**	1729	1152	
Total **Protein**	98	65	grams
Total **Carbohydrates**	340	226	grams
Total **Fat**	10	7	grams
Total **Saturated Fat**	1	1	grams
Total **Cholesterol**	0	0	milligrams
Total **Sodium**	4275	3205	milligrams
Total **Fiber**	50	33	grams
% **Calories from Fat**	5	5	

Bran Bread

Here, oat bran combines with wheat to make a soft, light wheat bread that slices like white bread but has a unique wheat flavor.

INGREDIENTS

1 1/2-Pound Recipe		1-Pound Recipe
2 teaspoons	**active dry yeast**	1 1/2 teaspoons
1 1/4 cups	**bread flour**	3/4 cup + 2 tablespoons
1 1/4 cups	**whole-wheat flour**	3/4 cup + 2 tablespoons
3/4 cup	**oat bran**	1/2 cup
1 1/2 teaspoons	**salt**	1 teaspoon
3 tablespoons	**brown sugar**	2 tablespoons
3 tablespoons	**butter**	2 tablespoons
9 ounces	**warm water**	6 ounces

NOTES:

1. For machines with yeast dispensers, use 3 1/2 teaspoons of yeast for the 1 1/2-pound loaf.
2. For a variation, try using bran instead of oat bran.

NUTRITIONAL ANALYSIS

	1 1/2-Pound	1-Pound	
Total **Calories**	1802	1199	
Total **Protein**	56	34	grams
Total **Carbohydrates**	312	208	grams
Total **Fat**	45	30	grams
Total **Saturated Fat**	23	15	grams
Total **Cholesterol**	93	62	milligrams
Total **Sodium**	3222	2148	milligrams
Total **Fiber**	32	21	grams
% **Calories from Fat**	22	22	

Cashew-Date Bread

This bread was created for cashew-nut lovers. The dates give the bread an exotic and sweet flavor that nicely complements that of the cashew nuts.

INGREDIENTS

1½-Pound Recipe		1-Pound Recipe
1½ teaspoons	**active dry yeast**	1 teaspoon
2 cups	**bread flour**	1⅓ cups
¼ cup	**chopped dates**	3 tablespoons
¼ cup	**raw cashew nuts (chopped)**	3 tablespoons
½ cup	**whole-wheat flour**	⅓ cup
½ teaspoon	**cinnamon**	¼ teaspoon
1 teaspoon	**salt**	½ teaspoon
3 tablespoons	**rolled oats**	2 tablespoons
2 tablespoons	**butter**	1½ tablespoons
3 tablespoons	**honey**	2 tablespoons
3 ounces	**warm buttermilk**	2 ounces
¾ cup	**warm water**	½ cup

NOTES:

1. For machines with yeast dispensers, use 3 teaspoons of yeast for the 1½-pound loaf.
2. If roasted, salted cashews are used, reduce the salt by ½ teaspoon.

NUTRITIONAL ANALYSIS

	1½-Pound	1-Pound	
Total **Calories**	2004	1375	
Total **Protein**	54	36	grams
Total **Carbohydrates**	346	233	grams
Total **Fat**	49	36	grams
Total **Saturated Fat**	17	13	grams
Total **Cholesterol**	70	52	milligrams
Total **Sodium**	2204	1115	milligrams
Total **Fiber**	18	12	grams
% **Calories from Fat**	22	24	

Challah Bread (Jewish Egg Bread)

• • •

see page 39

Buttermilk & Honey Bread

• • •

see page 46

Shredded-Wheat Nut Bread

• • •

see page 55

Raisin Walnut Bread

see page 54

Walnut Herb Bread

• • •

see page 58

Sunflower Potato Bread

• • •

see page 70

Whole-Wheat & Buckwheat Bread

• • •

see page 71

Whole-Wheat Three-Seed Bread

• • •

see page 78

Whole-Wheat Bagel Bread

• • •

see page 79

Pistachio Oatmeal Bread

see page 100

Millet Bread

• • •

see page 116

Pumpkin-Pie Bread

• • •

see page 134

Date-Molasses Bread

Dates, molasses, and a high percentage of whole-wheat flour make this slightly sweet bread a favorite for toast.

INGREDIENTS

1½-Pound Recipe		1-Pound Recipe
2 teaspoons	**active dry yeast**	1½ teaspoons
½ cup	**bread flour**	⅓ cup
2½ cups	**whole-wheat flour**	1⅔ cups
¾ cup	**dates (chopped)**	⅓ cup
½ teaspoon	**salt**	½ teaspoon
1 tablespoon	**butter**	½ tablespoon
½ cup	**warm milk**	3 ounces
2 tablespoons	**molasses**	1½ tablespoons
5 ounces	**warm water**	3½ ounces

NOTES:

1. For machines with yeast dispensers, use 4 teaspoons of yeast for the 1½-pound loaf.
2. If your machine is equipped with a whole-grain cycle, use it for this bread.
3. You may add the dates at the mix-cycle beep, if your machine is so equipped.

NUTRITIONAL ANALYSIS

	1½-Pound	1-Pound	
Total **Calories**	1918	1277	
Total **Protein**	58	39	grams
Total **Carbohydrates**	401	270	grams
Total **Fat**	20	12	grams
Total **Saturated Fat**	9	5	grams
Total **Cholesterol**	36	19	milligrams
Total **Sodium**	1169	1142	milligrams
Total **Fiber**	46	31	grams
% Calories from Fat	9	8	

Farmer's Bread

This is a traditional, crumbly textured whole-wheat bread. Dough conditioner (optional) can be added to give the bread a less crumbly texture, if desired.

INGREDIENTS

1 1/2-Pound Recipe		1-Pound Recipe
1 1/2 teaspoons	**active dry yeast**	1 teaspoon
1 cup	**bread flour**	3/4 cup
1/2 cup	**seedless raisins**	1/3 cup
1 tablespoon	**dough conditioner (optional)**	2 teaspoons
2 cups	**whole-wheat flour**	1 1/4 cup
1 teaspoon	**salt**	1/2 teaspoon
1 1/2 tablespoons	**brown sugar**	1 tablespoon
1 1/2 tablespoons	**butter**	1 tablespoon
9 ounces	**warm milk**	3/4 cup

NOTES:

1. For machines with yeast dispensers, use 3 teaspoons of yeast for the 1 1/2-pound loaf.
2. If your machine is equipped with a whole-grain cycle, use it for this bread.

NUTRITIONAL ANALYSIS

	1 1/2-Pound	1-Pound	
Total **Calories**	1878	1258	
Total **Protein**	62	41	grams
Total **Carbohydrates**	365	244	grams
Total **Fat**	27	18	grams
Total **Saturated Fat**	14	9	grams
Total **Cholesterol**	58	39	milligrams
Total **Sodium**	2293	1173	milligrams
Total **Fiber**	37	23	grams
% **Calories from Fat**	13	13	

Graham Bread

Graham flour's special milling process gives it a taste that's slightly sweeter than regular whole-wheat flour. That sweetness is evident in this light wheat bread.

WHEAT BREADS

INGREDIENTS

$1\frac{1}{2}$-Pound Recipe		1-Pound Recipe
1 teaspoon	**active dry yeast**	$\frac{1}{2}$ teaspoon
$2\frac{1}{4}$ cups + 3 tablespoons	**bread flour**	$1\frac{1}{2}$ cups + 2 tablespoons
$\frac{3}{4}$ cup	**graham flour**	$\frac{1}{2}$ cup
1 teaspoon	**salt**	$\frac{1}{2}$ teaspoon
$\frac{1}{3}$ cup	**dry milk**	$\frac{1}{4}$ cup
3 tablespoons	**brown sugar**	2 tablespoons
1	**egg**	1
$\frac{1}{2}$ cup	**warm milk**	3 ounces
$1\frac{1}{2}$ tablespoons	**molasses**	1 tablespoon
$1\frac{1}{2}$ tablespoons	**butter**	1 tablespoon
1 cup	**warm water**	5 ounces

NOTES:

1. For machines with yeast dispensers, use 2 teaspoons of yeast for the $1\frac{1}{2}$-pound loaf.
2. You may substitute whole-wheat flour for graham flour, if graham flour isn't available.

NUTRITIONAL ANALYSIS

	$1\frac{1}{2}$-Pound	1-Pound	
Total **Calories**	2094	1430	
Total **Protein**	70	50	grams
Total **Carbohydrates**	386	259	grams
Total **Fat**	30	21	grams
Total **Saturated Fat**	13	9	grams
Total **Cholesterol**	265	248	milligrams
Total **Sodium**	2403	1282	milligrams
Total **Fiber**	17	11	grams
% **Calories from Fat**	13	14	

Honey Wheat Bread

This traditional light wheat bread has the texture of white bread and a mild wheat taste.

INGREDIENTS

1 1/2-Pound Recipe		1-Pound Recipe
1 1/2 teaspoons	**active dry yeast**	1 teaspoon
1/2 teaspoon	**sugar**	1/2 teaspoon
2 cups	**bread flour**	1 1/3 cups
1 1/2 teaspoons	**salt**	1 1/2 teaspoons
1 1/4 cup	**whole-wheat flour**	3/4 cup
1	**egg**	1
1 1/2 tablespoons	**butter**	1 tablespoon
4 tablespoons	**honey**	2 tablespoons
1/2 cup	**warm milk**	1/4 cup
1/4 cup	**warm water**	1/4 cup

NOTE:
For machines with yeast dispensers, use 3 teaspoons of yeast for the 1 1/2-pound loaf.

NUTRITIONAL ANALYSIS

	1 1/2-Pound	1-Pound	
Total **Calories**	2033	1259	
Total **Protein**	65	42	grams
Total **Carbohydrates**	381	228	grams
Total **Fat**	31	22	grams
Total **Saturated Fat**	14	10	grams
Total **Cholesterol**	265	247	milligrams
Total **Sodium**	3331	2231	milligrams
Total **Fiber**	23	14	grams
% Calories from Fat	14	15	

Sesame Wheat Bread

This light wheat bread has a nutty sesame flavor. Try varying the amount of sesame seeds to suit your taste.

INGREDIENTS

$1^1/_2$-Pound Recipe		1-Pound Recipe
2 teaspoons	**active dry yeast**	$1^1/_2$ teaspoons
$2^1/_2$ cups	**bread flour**	$1^1/_2$ cups
$^3/_4$ cup	**whole-wheat flour**	$^1/_2$ cup
1 tablespoon	**sesame seeds**	2 teaspoons
$1^1/_2$ teaspoons	**salt**	1 teaspoon
1 tablespoon	**brown sugar**	2 teaspoons
2 tablespoons	**butter**	$1^1/_2$ tablespoons
3 ounces	**warm milk**	$^1/_4$ cup
$^3/_4$ cup	**warm water**	$^1/_2$ cup

NOTE:
For machines with yeast dispensers, use $3^1/_2$ teaspoons of yeast for the $1^1/_2$-pound loaf.

NUTRITIONAL ANALYSIS

	$1^1/_2$-Pound	1-Pound	
Total **Calories**	1774	1201	
Total **Protein**	56	38	grams
Total **Carbohydrates**	311	207	grams
Total **Fat**	35	25	grams
Total **Saturated Fat**	16	12	grams
Total **Cholesterol**	66	49	milligrams
Total **Sodium**	3259	2173	milligrams
Total **Fiber**	17	11	grams
% **Calories from Fat**	18	19	

Sunflower-Potato Bread

The mixture of potato flakes, sunflower seeds, and wheat gives this bread its hearty, whole-grain flavor.

INGREDIENTS

$1^1/_2$-Pound Recipe		1-Pound Recipe
2 teaspoons	**active dry yeast**	$1^1/_2$ teaspoons
3 tablespoons	**brown sugar**	2 tablespoons
2 cups	**bread flour**	$1^1/_3$ cups
3 tablespoons	**sunflower seeds**	2 tablespoons
1 cup	**whole-wheat flour**	$^2/_3$ cup
$1^1/_2$ teaspoons	**salt**	1 teaspoon
$^1/_2$ cup	**instant mashed-potato flakes or buds**	$^1/_3$ cup
3 tablespoons	**butter**	2 tablespoons
$1^1/_4$ cup	**warm water**	7 ounces

NOTE:
For machines with yeast dispensers, use $3^1/_2$ teaspoons of yeast for the $1^1/_2$-pound loaf.

NUTRITIONAL ANALYSIS

	$1^1/_2$-Pound	1-Pound	
Total **Calories**	2134	1422	
Total **Protein**	59	40	grams
Total **Carbohydrates**	350	234	grams
Total **Fat**	59	39	grams
Total **Saturated Fat**	24	16	grams
Total **Cholesterol**	93	62	milligrams
Total **Sodium**	3581	2385	milligrams
Total **Fiber**	20	14	grams
% **Calories from Fat**	25	25	

Whole-Wheat & Buckwheat Bread

This bread doesn't rise much, usually making a dense, flat loaf. If you like buckwheat, this is an excellent, densely textured bread.

INGREDIENTS

1½-Pound Recipe		1-Pound Recipe
2½ teaspoons	**active dry yeast**	2 teaspoons
1 cup	**buckwheat flour**	⅔ cup
2 cups	**whole-wheat flour**	1⅓ cups
1½ tablespoons	**wheat gluten (optional)**	1 tablespoon
2 teaspoons	**salt**	1 teaspoon
1 tablespoon	**brown sugar**	2 teaspoons
2 tablespoons	**butter**	1½ tablespoons
1½ tablespoons	**molasses**	1 tablespoon
¼ cup	**warm water**	1½ ounces
¾ cup	**warm milk**	½ cup

NOTES:

1. For machines with yeast dispensers, use 4½ teaspoons of yeast for the 1½-pound loaf.
2. For machines with low-power motors, add 2 tablespoons of warm water for the 1½-pound loaf
3. If your machine is equipped with a whole-grain cycle, use it for this bread.

NUTRITIONAL ANALYSIS

	1½-Pound	1-Pound	
Total **Calories**	1651	1120	
Total **Protein**	57	38	grams
Total **Carbohydrates**	304	203	grams
Total **Fat**	33	24	grams
Total **Saturated Fat**	17	13	grams
Total **Cholesterol**	70	52	milligrams
Total **Sodium**	4390	2217	milligrams
Total **Fiber**	31	21	grams
% **Calories from Fat**	18	19	

Whole-Wheat Buttermilk-Raisin Bread

This coarsely textured wheat bread has a slightly sweet taste. Add additional raisins, if you like.

INGREDIENTS

1½-Pound Recipe		1-Pound Recipe
2 teaspoons	**active dry yeast**	1½ teaspoons
½ cup	**bread flour**	½ cup
2½ cups	**whole-wheat flour**	1½ cups
6 tablespoons	**raisins**	¼ cup
½ teaspoon	**baking soda**	¼ teaspoon
1½ teaspoons	**salt**	1 teaspoon
2½ tablespoons	**butter**	1½ tablespoons
5 ounces	**buttermilk**	½ cup
2 tablespoons	**honey**	1½ tablespoons
¼ cup	**warm water**	2 tablespoons

NOTES:

1. For machines with yeast dispensers, use 3½ teaspoons of yeast for the 1½-pound loaf.
2. If your machine is equipped with a whole-grain cycle, use it for this bread.

NUTRITIONAL ANALYSIS

	1½-Pound	1-Pound	
Total **Calories**	1884	1275	
Total **Protein**	60	41	grams
Total **Carbohydrates**	353	242	grams
Total **Fat**	37	23	grams
Total **Saturated Fat**	20	12	grams
Total **Cholesterol**	90	57	milligrams
Total **Sodium**	3310	2220	milligrams
Total **Fiber**	42	26	grams
% Calories from Fat	18	16	

Whole-Wheat Cranberry Bread

Tart cranberries give this 100 percent-wheat bread a tangy flavor. It has a crumbly whole-wheat texture, which makes it excellent for toast.

INGREDIENTS

1½-Pound Recipe		1-Pound Recipe
2 teaspoons	**active dry yeast**	1½ teaspoons
3½ cups	**whole-wheat flour**	3½ cups + 2 tablespoons
½ cup	**whole cranberries**	⅓ cup
½ cup	**brown sugar**	⅓ cup
1½ teaspoons	**salt**	1 teaspoon
3 tablespoons	**molasses**	2 tablespoons
2 tablespoons	**butter**	1½ tablespoons
¾ cup	**warm water**	½ cup

NOTES:

1. For machines with yeast dispensers, use 3½ teaspoons of yeast for the 1½-pound loaf.
2. If your machine is equipped with a whole-grain cycle, use it for this bread.

NUTRITIONAL ANALYSIS

	1½-Pound	1-Pound	
Total **Calories**	2317	1576	
Total **Protein**	60	41	grams
Total **Carbohydrates**	477	321	grams
Total **Fat**	31	22	grams
Total **Saturated Fat**	16	12	grams
Total **Cholesterol**	62	47	milligrams
Total **Sodium**	3303	2202	milligrams
Total **Fiber**	54	36	grams
% **Calories from Fat**	12	13	

Whole-Wheat Egg Bread

This 100-percent wheat bread has a soft texture due to the eggs. Using maple syrup as a sweetener takes the edge off the sometimes slightly bitter taste of the whole wheat.

INGREDIENTS

1 1/2-Pound Recipe		1-Pound Recipe
3 teaspoons	**active dry yeast**	2 teaspoons
1 teaspoon	**sugar**	1/2 teaspoon
3 1/4 cups	**whole-wheat flour**	2 1/4 cups
2 teaspoons	**salt**	1 teaspoon
3	**eggs**	2
4 tablespoons	**olive oil**	2 1/2 tablespoons
4 tablespoons	**maple syrup**	2 1/2 tablespoons
3 ounces	**warm water**	1/4 cup

NOTES:

1. For machines with yeast dispensers, use 5 1/2 teaspoons of yeast for the 1 1/2-pound loaf.
2. If your machine is equipped with a whole-grain cycle, use it for this bread.
3. Because eggs vary in their effect on the consistency of the dough, be sure to watch the dough as it mixes. If it seems too runny, add flour, one tablespoon at a time, until the consistency is about right.

NUTRITIONAL ANALYSIS

	1 1/2-Pound	1-Pound	
Total **Calories**	2260	1510	
Total **Protein**	75	52	grams
Total **Carbohydrates**	344	233	grams
Total **Fat**	76	49	grams
Total **Saturated Fat**	13	9	grams
Total **Cholesterol**	639	426	milligrams
Total **Sodium**	4500	2288	milligrams
Total **Fiber**	50	35	grams
% **Calories from Fat**	30	29	

Whole-Wheat Potato Bread

If you like soft-textured whole-wheat bread, try this. The potato flakes soften the bread and give it a spongy texture.

INGREDIENTS

1$^1/_2$-Pound Recipe		1-Pound Recipe
2 teaspoons	**active dry yeast**	1$^1/_2$ teaspoons
2$^1/_4$ cups	**whole-wheat flour**	1$^3/_4$ cups
1 teaspoon	**cardamom**	$^1/_2$ teaspoon
3 tablespoons	**nonfat dry milk**	2 tablespoons
2 teaspoons	**salt**	1$^1/_2$ teaspoons
5 tablespoons	**instant mashed-potato flakes or buds**	3$^1/_2$ tablespoons
5 tablespoons	**brown sugar**	3$^1/_2$ tablespoons
1	**egg**	1
4 tablespoons	**butter**	2$^1/_2$ tablespoons
7 ounces	**warm water**	5 ounces

NOTES:

1. For machines with yeast dispensers, use 3$^1/_2$ teaspoons of yeast for the 1$^1/_2$-pound loaf.
2. If your machine is equipped with a whole-grain cycle, use it for this bread.

NUTRITIONAL ANALYSIS

	1$^1/_2$-Pound	1-Pound	
Total **Calories**	2260	1510	
Total **Protein**	75	52	grams
Total **Carbohydrates**	344	233	grams
Total **Fat**	76	49	grams
Total **Saturated Fat**	13	9	grams
Total **Cholesterol**	639	426	milligrams
Total **Sodium**	4500	2288	milligrams
Total **Fiber**	50	35	grams
% **Calories from Fat**	30	29	

Whole-Wheat Sally Lunn Bread

Because of its sweet flavor and whole-grain richness, this was my tasters' favorite 100-percent whole-wheat bread.

INGREDIENTS

1½-Pound Recipe		1-Pound Recipe
2 teaspoons	**active dry yeast**	1½ teaspoons
¼ teaspoon	**cream of tartar**	¼ teaspoon
1 teaspoon	**cardamom**	½ teaspoon
3¼ cups	**whole-wheat flour**	2 cups + 2 tablespoons
1 teaspoon	**salt**	½ teaspoon
½ cup + 1 tablespoon	**brown sugar**	6 tablespoons
2	**eggs**	1
4 tablespoons	**butter**	2½ tablespoons
7 ounces	**warm milk**	5 ounces

NOTES:

1. For machines with yeast dispensers, use 3½ teaspoons of yeast for the 1½-pound loaf.
2. If your machine is equipped with a whole-grain cycle, use it for this bread.

NUTRITIONAL ANALYSIS

	1½-Pound	1-Pound	
Total **Calories**	2435	1570	
Total **Protein**	75	48	grams
Total **Carbohydrates**	416	274	grams
Total **Fat**	65	40	grams
Total **Saturated Fat**	34	21	grams
Total **Cholesterol**	559	297	milligrams
Total **Sodium**	2411	1236	milligrams
Total **Fiber**	50	33	grams
% **Calories from Fat**	24	23	

Whole-Wheat Sourdough Bread

If you like both sourdough bread and wheat bread, try this. Sourdough adds a pungent flavor to this wheat bread. It's excellent topped with butter and honey.

INGREDIENTS

1½-Pound Recipe		1-Pound Recipe
1½ teaspoons	**active dry yeast**	1 teaspoon
1 cup	**bread flour**	½ cup
1 teaspoon	**salt**	½ teaspoon
2 cups	**whole-wheat flour**	1⅓ cups
¾ cup	**sourdough starter**	½ cup
1 cup	**warm water**	5 ounces
2 tablespoons	**honey**	1½ tablespoons

NOTES:

1. For machines with yeast dispensers, use 3 teaspoons of yeast for the 1½-pound loaf.
2. If you don't have sourdough starter, you can make your own. See page 156.
3. Because sourdough starter varies in consistency, check the dough when making. If it seems too runny, add flour, one tablespoon at a time. If it seems too stiff, add warm water, one tablespoon at a time.

NUTRITIONAL ANALYSIS

	1½-Pound	1-Pound	
Total **Calories**	1811	1217	
Total **Protein**	63	42	grams
Total **Carbohydrates**	382	257	grams
Total **Fat**	9	6	grams
Total **Saturated Fat**	1	1	grams
Total **Cholesterol**	0	0	milligrams
Total **Sodium**	2139	1071	milligrams
Total **Fiber**	34	23	grams
% **Calories from Fat**	4	4	

Whole-Wheat Three-Seed Bread

The three seeds (poppy, sunflower, and sesame) give a nutty flavor to this crunchy wheat-and-oatmeal bread. It's great for appetizer sandwiches. If you like seeds, you'll love this bread.

INGREDIENTS

1 1/2-Pound Recipe		1-Pound Recipe
2 teaspoons	**active dry yeast**	1 1/2 teaspoons
2 teaspoons	**gluten (optional)**	1 1/2 teaspoons
2 tablespoons	**sunflower seeds**	4 teaspoons
2 tablespoons	**sesame seeds**	4 teaspoons
2 tablespoons	**poppy seeds**	4 teaspoons
1/2 cup	**rolled oats**	1/4 cup
1 teaspoon	**salt**	1/2 teaspoon
2 cups	**whole-wheat flour**	1 1/2 cups
3 tablespoons	**olive oil**	2 tablespoons
2 tablespoons	**honey**	4 teaspoons
1 cup	**warm water**	5 1/2 ounces

NOTES:

1. For Panasonic/National machines, use 3 teaspoons of yeast for the 1 1/2-pound loaf.
2. Note that this bread has a slightly higher liquid content than other recipes. If you would like a stiffer, drier bread, add 2 extra tablespoons of whole-wheat flour.

NUTRITIONAL ANALYSIS

	1 1/2-Pound	1-Pound	
Total **Calories**	1748	1208	
Total **Protein**	51	36	grams
Total **Carbohydrates**	247	175	grams
Total **Fat**	72	48	grams
Total **Saturated Fat**	9	6	grams
Total **Cholesterol**	0	0	milligrams
Total **Sodium**	2147	1076	milligrams
Total **Fiber**	37	27	grams
% **Calories from Fat**	37	36	

Whole-Wheat Bagel Bread

If you don't feel like making bagels but want the texture of bagels with the low-fat nutritional benefits, try this bread. It tastes like a bagel and is especially good sliced and toasted.

INGREDIENTS

1 1/2-Pound Recipe		1-Pound Recipe
1 1/2 teaspoons	**active dry yeast**	1 teaspoon
1 1/2 teaspoons	**gluten**	1 teaspoon
3 cups	**whole-wheat flour**	2 cups
2 teaspoons	**salt**	1 1/2 teaspoons
3 tablespoons	**honey**	2 tablespoons
1 tablespoon	**warm water**	5 1/2 ounces

NOTE:
For Panasonic/National machines, use 3 teaspoons of yeast for the 1 1/2-pound loaf.

NUTRITIONAL ANALYSIS

	1 1/2-Pound	1-Pound	
Total **Calories**	1437	1030	
Total **Protein**	54	38	grams
Total **Carbohydrates**	313	226	grams
Total **Fat**	7	5	grams
Total **Saturated Fat**	1	1	grams
Total **Cholesterol**	0	0	milligrams
Total **Sodium**	4269	3202	milligrams
Total **Fiber**	46	31	grams
% **Calories from Fat**	4	4	

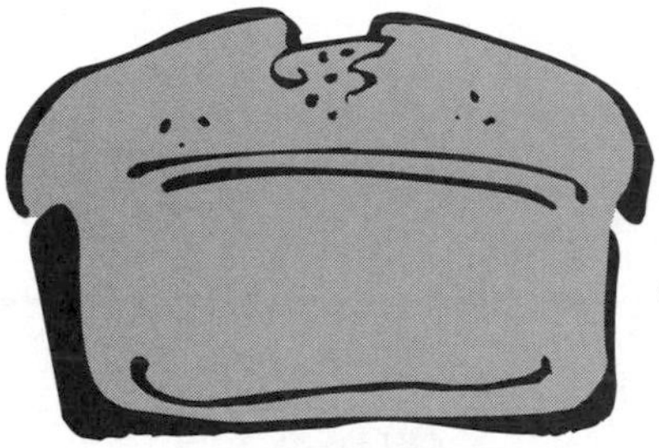

RYE BREADS

The distinctive taste of rye bread is loved the world over. Featured in this section are interesting variations on "standard" rye breads. As you bake rye breads in your bread machine, remember that the dough ball will usually be somewhat stiff and that rye breads don't rise much, giving them their uniquely dense texture.

German Rye Bread

If you like rye bread, you will love this authentic German country rye. Like all ryes, it has a dense texture and the distinctive taste of rye and caraway.

INGREDIENTS

1½-Pound Recipe		1-Pound Recipe
1 tablespoon	**active dry yeast**	2 teaspoons
1 tablespoon	**caraway seeds**	2 teaspoons
2¼ cups	**bread flour**	1½ cups
1½ teaspoons	**salt**	1 teaspoon
2½ tablespoons	**unsweetened cocoa**	5 teaspoons
1½ cups	**rye flour**	1 cup
2¼ cups	**warm water**	7 ounces
1½ tablespoons	**butter**	1 tablespoon
2½ tablespoons	**molasses**	5 teaspoons

NOTE:
For Panasonic/National machines, use 3½ teaspoons of yeast for the 1½-pound loaf.

NUTRITIONAL ANALYSIS

	1½-Pound	1-Pound	
Total **Calories**	2136	1423	
Total **Protein**	72	48	grams
Total **Carbohydrates**	403	269	grams
Total **Fat**	30	20	grams
Total **Saturated Fat**	12	8	grams
Total **Cholesterol**	47	31	milligrams
Total **Sodium**	3250	2167	milligrams
Total **Fiber**	10	6	grams
% **Calories from Fat**	13	13	

Buckwheat Rye Bread

Due to the small amount of wheat flour used, this bread doesn't rise much. The result, however, is a bread with a dense texture and strong buckwheat flavor that will please buckwheat lovers.

INGREDIENTS

1½-Pound Recipe		1-Pound Recipe
2 teaspoons	**active dry yeast**	1½ teaspoons
1½ tablespoons	**gluten powder**	1 tablespoon
1 tablespoon	**brown sugar**	½ tablespoon
1½ cups	**rye flour**	1 cup
¼ teaspoon	**ground cloves**	⅛ teaspoon
1 cup	**whole-wheat flour**	⅔ cup
½ cup	**buckwheat flour**	⅓ cup
1 teaspoon	**salt**	½ teaspoon
3 tablespoons	**molasses**	2 tablespoons
2 tablespoons	**butter**	1 tablespoon
1 cup + 2 tablespoons	**warm water**	¾ cup

NOTES:

1. For machines with yeast dispensers, use 4 teaspoons of yeast for the 1½-pound loaf.
2. If your machine is equipped with a whole-grain cycle, use it for this bread.

NUTRITIONAL ANALYSIS

	1½-Pound	1-Pound	
Total **Calories**	1670	1072	
Total **Protein**	52	35	grams
Total **Carbohydrates**	312	206	grams
Total **Fat**	31	17	grams
Total **Saturated Fat**	15	8	grams
Total **Cholesterol**	62	31	milligrams
Total **Sodium**	2192	1105	milligrams
Total **Fiber**	39	26	grams
% **Calories from Fat**	16	14	

Dijon Rye Bread

This mild rye has a tangy flavor. It's densely textured and doesn't rise much, but it's a great bread for sandwiches. Dijon mustard is made from white wine, vinegar, spices, and ground mustard seed, and it complements the rye flavor quite well.

INGREDIENTS

1 1/2-Pound Recipe		1-Pound Recipe
1 1/2 teaspoons	**active dry yeast**	1 teaspoon
1 tablespoon	**gluten powder**	2 teaspoons
2 teaspoons	**sugar**	1 1/8 teaspoons
2 1/4 cups	**bread flour**	1 1/2 cups
1/2 cup	**rye flour**	1/3 cup
4 1/2 tablespoons	**oat bran**	3 tablespoons
1 1/2 teaspoons	**ground caraway seeds**	1 teaspoon
1 1/2 teaspoons	**salt**	1 teaspoon
4 1/2 tablespoons	**Dijon mustard**	3 tablespoons
2 1/2 tablespoons	**molasses**	1 1/2 tablespoons
2 tablespoons	**olive oil**	1 1/2 tablespoons
7 ounces	**warm water**	4 1/2 ounces

NOTES:
1. For machines with yeast dispensers, use 3 teaspoons of yeast for the 1 1/2-pound loaf.
2. For machines with low-power motors, add 2 tablespoons of warm water for the 1-pound loaf.
3. If your machine is equipped with a whole-grain cycle, use it for this bread.

NUTRITIONAL ANALYSIS

	1 1/2-Pound	1-Pound	
Total **Calories**	1862	1252	
Total **Protein**	56	37	grams
Total **Carbohydrates**	328	216	grams
Total **Fat**	36	26	grams
Total **Saturated Fat**	5	3	grams
Total **Cholesterol**	0	0	milligrams
Total **Sodium**	3245	2161	milligrams
Total **Fiber**	17	11	grams
% **Calories from Fat**	17	19	

Dill Rye Bread

This light rye has a spicy flavor. It's excellent as a sandwich bread.

INGREDIENTS

1½-Pound Recipe		1-Pound Recipe
1½ teaspoons	**active dry yeast**	1 teaspoon
1½ tablespoons	**brown sugar**	1 tablespoon
½ teaspoon	**caraway seeds**	½ teaspoon
½ tablespoon	**dill seeds**	1 teaspoon
2¼ cups	**bread flour**	1½ cups
1 teaspoon	**salt**	½ teaspoon
½ tablespoon	**dill weed**	1 teaspoon
4 tablespoons	**nonfat dry milk**	2½ tablespoons
¾ cup	**rye flour**	½ cup
1½ tablespoons	**butter**	1 tablespoon
9 ounces	**warm water**	¾ cup

NOTE:
For machines with yeast dispensers, use 3 teaspoons of yeast for the 1½-pound loaf.

NUTRITIONAL ANALYSIS

	1½-Pound	1-Pound	
Total **Calories**	1720	1144	
Total **Protein**	55	36	grams
Total **Carbohydrates**	319	213	grams
Total **Fat**	25	16	grams
Total **Saturated Fat**	12	8	grams
Total **Cholesterol**	51	34	milligrams
Total **Sodium**	2276	1157	milligrams
Total **Fiber**	17	12	grams
% Calories from Fat	13	13	

Oat Rye Bread

This bread has a soft, but dense, texture and a mild rye flavor. The loaf won't rise much and will stay fairly small.

INGREDIENTS

1 1/2-Pound Recipe		1-Pound Recipe
2 teaspoons	**active dry yeast**	1 1/2 teaspoons
1 1/4 cups	**bread flour**	3/4 cup
1 1/2 teaspoons	**ground caraway seeds**	1 teaspoon
1 1/2 cups	**rye flour**	1 cup
1/4 cup	**oat flour**	1/4 cup
1 teaspoon	**salt**	1/2 teaspoon
1	**egg**	1
1 1/2 tablespoons	**butter**	1 tablespoon
1 1/2 tablespoons	**molasses**	1 tablespoon
6 1/2 ounces	**warm water**	1/2 cup
2 teaspoons	**dough enhancer (optional)**	1/2 tablespoon

NOTES:

1. For machines with yeast dispensers, use 4 teaspoons of yeast for the 1 1/2-pound loaf.
2. If your machine is equipped with a whole-grain cycle, use it for this bread.

NUTRITIONAL ANALYSIS

	1 1/2-Pound	1-Pound	
Total **Calories**	1600	1085	
Total **Protein**	48	34	grams
Total **Carbohydrates**	289	192	grams
Total **Fat**	29	21	grams
Total **Saturated Fat**	13	9	grams
Total **Cholesterol**	260	244	milligrams
Total **Sodium**	2229	1152	milligrams
Total **Fiber**	30	21	grams
% **Calories from Fat**	16	17	

Swedish Rye Bread

Fennel seeds and orange juice give this traditional rye bread its distinctive flavor.

INGREDIENTS

1½-Pound Recipe		1-Pound Recipe
1½ teaspoons	**active dry yeast**	1 teaspoon
2 teaspoons	**fennel seeds**	1 teaspoon
½ teaspoon	**sugar**	½ teaspoon
2 cups	**bread flour**	1⅓ cups
1 cup	**rye flour**	⅔ cup
1½ teaspoons	**salt**	1 teaspoon
1 tablespoon	**olive oil**	½ tablespoon
4 tablespoons	**molasses**	2½ tablespoons
3 ounces	**orange juice**	2 ounces
3 ounces	**warm milk**	2 ounces
2 tablespoons	**warm water**	1½ tablespoons

NOTES:

1. For machines with yeast dispensers, use 3 teaspoons of yeast for the 1½-pound loaf.
2. For machines with low-power motors, add 2 tablespoons of warm water for the 1½-pound loaf.

NUTRITIONAL ANALYSIS

	1½-Pound	1-Pound	
Total **Calories**	1808	1178	
Total **Protein**	48	32	grams
Total **Carbohydrates**	352	233	grams
Total **Fat**	21	12	grams
Total **Saturated Fat**	3	2	grams
Total **Cholesterol**	4	3	milligrams
Total **Sodium**	3313	2206	milligrams
Total **Fiber**	20	13	grams
% **Calories from Fat**	11	9	

Corn Rye Bread

A must for rye lovers. Corn Rye is a wonderful, light variation of rye bread with the crunchiness of corn and the flavor of rye, wheat, and caraway.

INGREDIENTS

1½-Pound Recipe		1-Pound Recipe
1½ teaspoons	**active dry yeast**	1 teaspoon
1 teaspoon	**dough enhancer (optional)**	½ teaspoon
2 teaspoons	**caraway seeds**	1½ teaspoons
2½ tablespoons	**sesame seeds**	5 teaspoons
¼ cup	**rye flour**	2 tablespoons
¼ cup	**cornmeal**	2 tablespoons
2½ cups	**whole-wheat flour**	1¾ cups
½ teaspoon	**salt**	¼ teaspoon
4 tablespoons	**molasses**	2½ tablespoons
2 teaspoons	**olive oil**	1½ teaspoons
2 teaspoons	**molasses**	1½ teaspoons
1 cup	**warm water**	¾ cup

NOTES:
1. For Panasonic/National machines, use 2½ teaspoons of yeast for the 1½-pound loaf.
2. For DAK/Welbilt machines, add 2 tablespoons of warm water to the 1½-pound loaf.

NUTRITIONAL ANALYSIS

	1½-Pound	1-Pound	
Total **Calories**	1506	1013	
Total **Protein**	54	36	grams
Total **Carbohydrates**	281	188	grams
Total **Fat**	28	20	grams
Total **Saturated Fat**	4	3	grams
Total **Cholesterol**	0	0	milligrams
Total **Sodium**	1094	551	milligrams
Total **Fiber**	44	30	grams
% **Calories from Fat**	17	17	

Russian Black Bread

This is a complete meal in a loaf. In fact, the story goes that during the siege of Leningrad, Russian black bread was all the Russians had to eat. It is nutritious and a must-try for rye lovers.

INGREDIENTS

1½-Pound Recipe		1-Pound Recipe
2 teaspoons	**active dry yeast**	1½ teaspoons
¼ teaspoon	**ground fennel seed**	¼ teaspoon
1 teaspoon	**dried onion**	½ teaspoon
2 teaspoons	**ground caraway**	1½ teaspoons
¾ cup	**All-Bran cereal**	½ cup
1 teaspoon	**salt**	½ teaspoon
½ teaspoon	**sugar**	½ teaspoon
1 cup	**bread flour**	¾ cup
1¼ cups	**rye flour**	¾ cup
2 tablespoons	**butter**	1½ tablespoons
1½ tablespoons	**unsweetened cocoa**	1 tablespoon
¼ cup	**molasses**	2½ tablespoons
1 tablespoon	**vinegar**	2 teaspoons
¾ cup	**warm water**	½ cup

NOTE:
For Panasonic/National machines, use 3½ teaspoons of yeast for the 1½-pound loaf.

NUTRITIONAL ANALYSIS

	1½-Pound	1-Pound	
Total **Calories**	1688	1146	
Total **Protein**	53	36	grams
Total **Carbohydrates**	326	218	grams
Total **Fat**	34	24	grams
Total **Saturated Fat**	15	11	grams
Total **Cholesterol**	62	47	milligrams
Total **Sodium**	2788	1502	milligrams
Total **Fiber**	29	19	grams
% **Calories from Fat**	18	19	

Onion Rye Bread

The taste of toasted onion combined with rye made this bread the favorite of my rye-loving bread testers. It makes an excellent bread for a ham-and-cheese sandwich.

INGREDIENTS

1 1/2-Pound Recipe		1-Pound Recipe
1 1/2 teaspoons	**active dry yeast**	1 teaspoon
1 teaspoon	**caraway seeds**	1 teaspoon
1 cup	**bread flour**	3/4 cup
3 tablespoons	**onion soup mix**	2 tablespoons
1 cup	**rye flour**	3/4 cup
1 cup	**whole-wheat flour**	1/2 cup
1 tablespoon	**butter**	1 tablespoon
2 tablespoons	**milk**	4 teaspoons
1 tablespoon	**olive oil**	2 teaspoons
1 tablespoon	**vinegar**	2 teaspoons
1/4 cup	**molasses**	2 1/2 tablespoons
2 teaspoons	**vinegar**	1 1/2 teaspoons
3/4 cup	**warm water**	1/2 cup

NOTE:
For Panasonic/National machines, use 3 1/2 teaspoons of yeast for the 1 1/2-pound loaf.

NUTRITIONAL ANALYSIS

	1 1/2-Pound	1-Pound	
Total **Calories**	1688	1146	
Total **Protein**	53	36	grams
Total **Carbohydrates**	326	218	grams
Total **Fat**	34	24	grams
Total **Saturated Fat**	15	11	grams
Total **Cholesterol**	62	47	milligrams
Total **Sodium**	2788	1502	milligrams
Total **Fiber**	29	19	grams
% **Calories from Fat**	18	19	

Pumpernickel Bread

The traditional taste of pumpernickel is a favorite of rye-bread lovers. With its dense rye texture, this bread is excellent when sliced thin for deli-type sandwiches.

INGREDIENTS

1½-Pound Recipe		1-Pound Recipe
2½ teaspoons	**active dry yeast**	2 teaspoons
1½ cups	**bread flour**	1 cup
1½ cups	**rye flour**	1 cup
1½ teaspoons	**salt**	1 teaspoon
1 tablespoon	**caraway seed**	2 teaspoons
1 tablespoon	**butter**	1 tablespoon
2 tablespoons	**molasses**	2½ teaspoons
6½ ounces	**warm water**	4½ ounces

NOTES:

1. For Panasonic/National machines, use 4 teaspoons of yeast for the 1½-pound loaf.
2. For DAK/Welbilt machines, use 7½ ounces of warm water for the 1½-pound loaf.

NUTRITIONAL ANALYSIS

	1½-Pound	1-Pound	
Total **Calories**	1744	1188	
Total **Protein**	55	37	grams
Total **Carbohydrates**	343	226	grams
Total **Fat**	21	18	grams
Total **Saturated Fat**	8	8	grams
Total **Cholesterol**	31	31	milligrams
Total **Sodium**	3268	2177	milligrams
Total **Fiber**	8	5	grams
% **Calories from Fat**	11	14	

CORN BREADS

The three recipes in this section feature the staple grain of the Western Hemisphere: corn. Each of these recipes is a different variation of the use of corn in yeast bread, and you'll find each to be delightful in its own way.

Cornmeal-Honey Bread

This simple bread has a white-bread look with a corb-bread crunch.

INGREDIENTS

$1^1/_2$-Pound Recipe		1-Pound Recipe
$1^1/_2$ teaspoons	**active dry yeast**	1 teaspoon
3 cups	**bread flour**	2 cups
$^1/_2$ cup	**cornmeal**	$^1/_3$ cup
$1^1/_2$ teaspoons	**salt**	1 teaspoon
3 tablespoons	**honey**	2 tablespoons
1 tablespoon	**butter**	$^1/_2$ tablespoon
$^3/_4$ cup	**warm buttermilk**	$^1/_2$ cup
3 ounces	**warm water**	$^1/_4$ cup

NOTE:
For machines with yeast dispensers, use 3 teaspoons of yeast for the $1^1/_2$-pound loaf.

NUTRITIONAL ANALYSIS

	$1^1/_2$-Pound	1-Pound	
Total **Calories**	2084	1371	
Total **Protein**	63	42	grams
Total **Carbohydrates**	405	270	grams
Total **Fat**	22	13	grams
Total **Saturated Fat**	9	5	grams
Total **Cholesterol**	47	26	milligrams
Total **Sodium**	3345	2230	milligrams
Total **Fiber**	13	9	grams
% **Calories from Fat**	9	8	

Southwestern Pumpkin Bread

Punpkin, a staple vegetable in Latin America, is good with Mexican food, such as refried beans, or Southwestern fare. Both the pumpkin and the corn give this bread a rich yellow color.

INGREDIENTS

1½-Pound Recipe		1-Pound Recipe
1½ teaspoons	**active dry yeast**	1 teaspoon
3 cups	**bread flour**	2 cups
¼ cup	**cornmeal**	2 tablespoons
1½ teaspoons	**salt**	1 teaspoon
¼ cup	**brown sugar**	2 tablespoons
½ cup	**canned pumpkin**	½ cup
1	**egg**	1
5 ounces	**warm water**	2½ ounces

NOTE:
For machines with yeast dispensers, use 3 teaspoons of yeast for the 1½-pound loaf.

NUTRITIONAL ANALYSIS

	1½-Pound	1-Pound	
Total **Calories**	1920	1252	
Total **Protein**	60	42	grams
Total **Carbohydrates**	366	245	grams
Total **Fat**	13	10	grams
Total **Saturated Fat**	3	2	grams
Total **Cholesterol**	213	213	milligrams
Total **Sodium**	3296	2214	milligrams
Total **Fiber**	10	6	grams
% Calories from Fat	6	7	

White Corn Bread

This crunchy bread has great look and texture. Try it with soup.

INGREDIENTS

1 1/2-Pound Recipe		1-Pound Recipe
1 1/2 teaspoons	**active dry yeast**	1 teaspoon
1/4 cup	**brown sugar**	3 tablespoons
2 1/4 cups + 2 tablespoons	**bread flour**	1 1/2 cups + 2 tablespoons
2 teaspoons	**salt**	1 1/2 teaspoons
1 cup	**white cornmeal**	3/4 cup
2	**eggs**	1
2 tablespoons	**butter**	1 1/2 tablespoons
7 ounces	**warm milk**	5 ounces

NOTES:

1. For machines with yeast dispensers, use 3 teaspoons of yeast for the 1 1/2-pound loaf.
2. Yellow cornmeal may be substituted for white cornmeal.

NUTRITIONAL ANALYSIS

	1 1/2-Pound	1-Pound	
Total **Calories**	2519	1549	
Total **Protein**	78	46	grams
Total **Carbohydrates**	446	273	grams
Total **Fat**	46	31	grams
Total **Saturated Fat**	20	14	grams
Total **Cholesterol**	497	266	milligrams
Total **Sodium**	4566	3385	milligrams
Total **Fiber**	20	13	grams
% **Calories from Fat**	17	18	

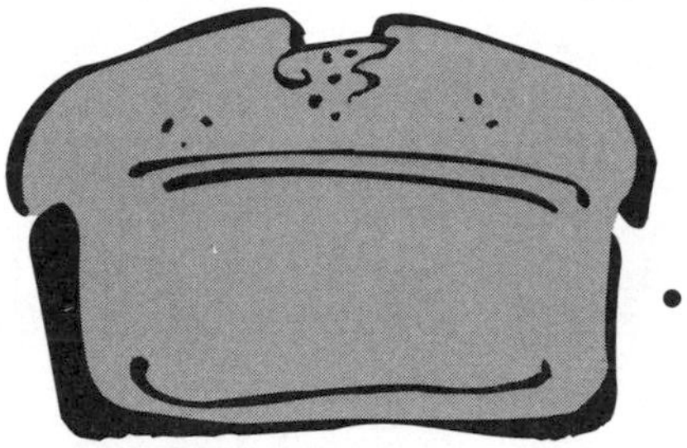

OAT BREADS

The breads in this section all include rolled oats in their recipes. Rolled oats (oatmeal) give the bread a soft, spongy texture and good, rich flavor, not to mention additional nutritional benefits. Oatmeal lovers will find that the variety of other ingredients used in the recipes complements the oat flavor and texture, producing some interesting breads.

Oatmeal-Sesame Bread

I keep getting repeat requests for this one. It has the spongy texture of oatmeal bread with the nutty taste of sesame seeds. It's a great sandwich bread.

INGREDIENTS

1 1/2-Pound Recipe		1-Pound Recipe
1 1/2 teaspoons	**active dry yeast**	1 teaspoon
2 1/4 cups	**bread flour**	1 3/4 cups
1 teaspoon	**salt**	1/2 teaspoon
4 tablespoons	**brown sugar**	2 1/2 tablespoons
8 tablespoons	**sesame seeds**	5 tablespoons
6 tablespoons	**rolled oats**	1/4 cup
2 tablespoons	**butter**	1 1/2 tablespoons
9 ounces	**warm water**	3/4 cup

NOTE:
For Panasonic/National machines, use 3 teaspoons of yeast for the 1 1/2-pound loaf.

NUTRITIONAL ANALYSIS

	1 1/2-Pound	1-Pound	
Total **Calories**	2308	1489	
Total **Protein**	64	41	grams
Total **Carbohydrates**	365	232	grams
Total **Fat**	67	45	grams
Total **Saturated Fat**	20	14	grams
Total **Cholesterol**	62	47	milligrams
Total **Sodium**	2167	1088	milligrams
Total **Fiber**	12	8	grams
% **Calories from Fat**	26	27	

Nebraska Oatmeal Bread

This traditional oatmeal bread is easy to make, uses basic ingredients, and is tasty and nutritious. The loaf is fairly densely textured.

INGREDIENTS

1½-Pound Recipe		1-Pound Recipe
1½ teaspoons	**active dry yeast**	1 teaspoon
2½ tablespoons	**brown sugar**	1½ tablespoons
2 cups	**bread flour**	1⅓ cups
1½ teaspoons	**salt**	1 teaspoon
1 cup	**rolled oats**	⅔ cup
1 tablespoon	**butter**	1 tablespoon
1 cup	**warm milk**	5 ounces
¼ cup	**warm water**	2 tablespoons

NOTES:

1. For machines with yeast dispensers, use 3 teaspoons of yeast for the 1½-pound loaf.
2. For a light-texture loaf, add an extra ½ teaspoon of yeast and an extra tablespoon of warm water for the 1½-pound recipe. Add ¼ teaspoon of yeast and 1½ tablespoon of water for the 1-pound loaf.

NUTRITIONAL ANALYSIS

	1½-Pound	1-Pound	
Total **Calories**	1641	1114	
Total **Protein**	55	37	grams
Total **Carbohydrates**	299	197	grams
Total **Fat**	24	20	grams
Total **Saturated Fat**	10	9	grams
Total **Cholesterol**	41	37	milligrams
Total **Sodium**	3341	2222	milligrams
Total **Fiber**	13	9	grams
% **Calories from Fat**	13	16	

Pistachio Oatmeal Bread

The distinctive flavor of pistachio nuts permeates this loaf. To get the best distribution of the pistachio oil in the dough, add the nuts at the beginning rather than at the mix-cycle beep

INGREDIENTS

1 1/2-Pound Recipe		**1-Pound Recipe**
1 1/2 teaspoons	**active dry yeast**	1 teaspoon
3/4 cup	**rolled oats**	3 tablespoons
2 1/2 cups	**bread flour**	1 2/3 cups
1 teaspoon	**salt**	1/2 teaspoon
1 teaspoon	**sugar**	1/2 teaspoon
1 1/2 tablespoons	**butter**	1 tablespoon
3 tablespoons	**honey**	2 tablespoons
3/4 cup	**warm milk**	1/2 cup
3 ounces	**warm water**	1/4 cup
1/3 cup	**chopped pistachio nuts**	1/4 cup

NOTES:
For machines with yeast dispensers, use 3 teaspoons of yeast for the 1 1/2-pound loaf.

NUTRITIONAL ANALYSIS

	1 1/2-Pound	**1-Pound**	
Total **Calories**	2157	1460	
Total **Protein**	64	43	grams
Total **Carbohydrates**	359	239	grams
Total **Fat**	53	38	grams
Total **Saturated Fat**	15	11	grams
Total **Cholesterol**	54	36	milligrams
Total **Sodium**	2239	1138	milligrams
Total **Fiber**	14	9	grams
% Calories from Fat	22	23	

Soy Oatmeal Bread

The addition of soy flour to this oatmeal bread boosts the nutritional level of the bread, particularly the protein content. This is a good low-fat bread.

INGREDIENTS

$1^1/_2$-Pound Recipe		1-Pound Recipe
1 teaspoon	**active dry yeast**	$^1/_2$ teaspoon
$^1/_3$ cup	**soy flour**	$^1/_4$ cup
$1^3/_4$ cups	**bread flour**	$1^1/_4$ cups
$1^1/_4$ cups	**rolled oats**	$^3/_4$ cup
$^1/_2$ teaspoon	**salt**	$^1/_4$ teaspoon
$1^1/_2$ tablespoons	**butter**	1 tablespoon
5 tablespoons	**molasses**	3 teaspoons
7 ounces	**warm water**	5 ounces

NOTE:
For machines with yeast dispensers, use 2 teaspoons of yeast for the $1^1/_2$-pound loaf and 1 teaspoon for the 1-pound loaf.

NUTRITIONAL ANALYSIS

	$1^1/_2$-Pound	1-Pound	
Total **Calories**	1821	1218	
Total **Protein**	62	43	grams
Total **Carbohydrates**	325	217	grams
Total **Fat**	28	18	grams
Total **Saturated Fat**	12	8	grams
Total **Cholesterol**	47	31	milligrams
Total **Sodium**	1158	589	milligrams
Total **Fiber**	16	10	grams
% **Calories from Fat**	14	14	

Sunflower Oatmeal Bread

The sunflower seeds secrete an oil that mixes throughout the dough and gives this bread a fine, nutty flavor. It's excellent for breakfast toast.

INGREDIENTS

1 1/2-Pound Recipe		1-Pound Recipe
1 1/2 teaspoons	**active dry yeast**	1 teaspoon
2 1/4 cups	**bread flour**	1 1/2 cups
1/4 cup	**sunflower seeds**	2 tablespoons
1 teaspoon	**salt**	1/2 teaspoon
1/4 cup	**rolled oats**	2 tablespoons
1/2 cup	**whole-wheat flour**	1/2 cup
1/2 teaspoon	**sugar**	1/2 teaspoon
1	**egg**	1
1 tablespoon	**butter**	1 tablespoon
1 tablespoon	**molasses**	1/2 tablespoon
1 1/2 tablespoons	**honey**	1/2 tablespoon
3 ounces	**warm buttermilk**	1/4 cup
1/2 cup	**warm water**	3 ounces

NOTES:

1. For machines with yeast dispensers, use 3 teaspoons of yeast for the 1 1/2-pound loaf.
2. Sunflower seeds may be added at the mix-cycle beep, if your machine is so equipped.

NUTRITIONAL ANALYSIS

	1 1/2-Pound	1-Pound	
Total **Calories**	1969	1387	
Total **Protein**	66	48	grams
Total **Carbohydrates**	336	233	grams
Total **Fat**	41	30	grams
Total **Saturated Fat**	12	11	grams
Total **Cholesterol**	252	249	milligrams
Total **Sodium**	2278	1182	milligrams
Total **Fiber**	15	12	grams
% **Calories from Fat**	19	20	

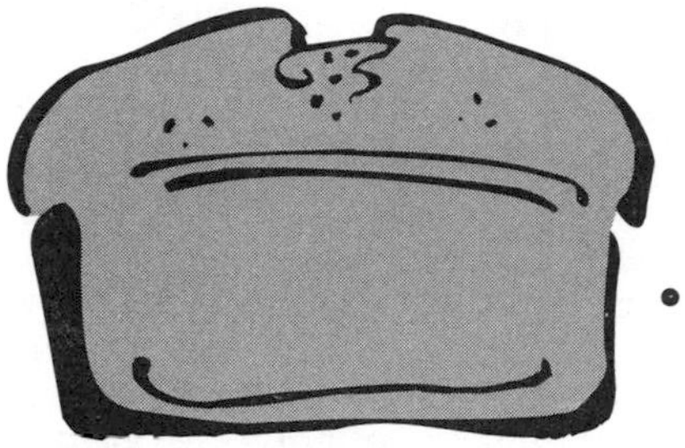

WHOLE-GRAIN BREADS

The breads in this section are characterized by the use of whole-grain flours of all types. These tasty breads are among the most nutritious you can bake. If you purchased your bread machine to make healthful breads, take a close look at the recipes in this section.

Seven-Grain Bread

This bread is one of my family's favorites because of its crunchy texture and 100-percent wheat flavor. The addition of the dough enhancer will give the bread a smoother texture, but it is excellent either way.

INGREDIENTS

1½-Pound Recipe		1-Pound Recipe
3 teaspoons	**active dry yeast**	2 teaspoons
1 tablespoon	**dough enhancer (optional)**	2 teaspoons
3 cups	**whole-wheat flour**	2 cups
2	**eggs**	1
1 teaspoon	**salt**	½ teaspoon
½ cup	**seven-grain cereal**	5 tablespoons
4 tablespoons	**honey**	3 tablespoons
3 tablespoons	**olive oil**	5 ounces
1 cup	**warm water**	1 tablespoon

NOTE:
Soak the seven-grain cereal in the water for 30-60 minutes before adding to recipe.

NUTRITIONAL ANALYSIS

	1½-Pound	1-Pound	
Total **Calories**	2149	1421	
Total **Protein**	71	45	grams
Total **Carbohydrates**	356	242	grams
Total **Fat**	59	38	grams
Total **Saturated Fat**	10	6	grams
Total **Cholesterol**	426	213	milligrams
Total **Sodium**	2265	1134	milligrams
Total **Fiber**	53	35	grams
% Calories from Fat	25	24	

Tri-Grain Bread

A hearty combination of barley, oats, and wheat makes this bread an excellent choice for breakfast toast or sandwiches. It has a strong grain flavor and is a whole-grain lover's delight.

INGREDIENTS

1 1/2-Pound Recipe		1-Pound Recipe
1 tablespoon	**active dry yeast**	2 teaspoons
1 tablespoon	**dough enhancer (optional)**	2 teaspoons
1 1/2 teaspoons	**gluten (optional)**	1 teaspoon
2 1/4 cups	**bread flour**	1 1/2 cups
4 1/2 tablespoons	**oat flour**	3 tablespoons
1/4 cup	**barley flour**	5 teaspoons
5 tablespoons	**wheat germ**	3 tablespoons
1 1/2 teaspoons	**salt**	1 teaspoon
3 teaspoons	**brown sugar**	2 teaspoons
2 tablespoons	**butter**	1 1/2 tablespoons
1 cup	**warm water**	5 ounces

NOTES:

1. For Panasonic/National machines, use 3 1/2 teaspoons of yeast for the 1 1/2-pound loaf.
2. For DAK/Welbilt machines, add 2 extra tablespoons of water for the 1 1/2-pound loaf.

NUTRITIONAL ANALYSIS

	1 1/2-Pound	1-Pound	
Total **Calories**	1728	1203	
Total **Protein**	59	38	grams
Total **Carbohydrates**	302	213	grams
Total **Fat**	34	24	grams
Total **Saturated Fat**	15	11	grams
Total **Cholesterol**	62	47	milligrams
Total **Sodium**	3216	2149	milligrams
Total **Fiber**	18	11	grams
% Calories from Fat	18	18	

Quinoa Bread

The nutty flavor of quinoa flour is evident in this high-protein loaf. Quinoa is the grain of the ancient Incas and has been a staple in South America for centuries. It has one of the highest protein contents of any of the grains.

INGREDIENTS

1½-Pound Recipe		1-Pound Recipe
1½ teaspoons	**active dry yeast**	1 teaspoon
1½ tablespoons	**dry milk**	1 tablespoon
3 tablespoons	**sugar**	2 tablespoons
1½ teaspoons	**salt**	1 teaspoon
½ cup	**quinoa flour**	¼ cup
½ cup	**whole-wheat flour**	¼ cup
2 cups	**bread flour**	1½ cups
1½ tablespoons	**butter**	1 tablespoon
9 ounces	**warm water**	¾ cup

NOTES:
For Panasonic/National machines, use 2 teaspoons of yeast for the 1½-pound loaf.

NUTRITIONAL ANALYSIS

	1½-Pound	1-Pound	
Total **Calories**	1841	1223	
Total **Protein**	57	37	grams
Total **Carbohydrates**	342	228	grams
Total **Fat**	28	18	grams
Total **Saturated Fat**	12	8	grams
Total **Cholesterol**	48	32	milligrams
Total **Sodium**	3253	2169	milligrams
Total **Fiber**	12	7	grams
% **Calories from Fat**	14	13	

Buckwheat-Barley Bread

This bread features the distinctive tastes of barley and buckwheat. It is a light whole-grain bread with a texture approaching that of white bread. Try making a tuna sandwich with it or having it with chicken soup.

INGREDIENTS

1 1/2-Pound Recipe		1-Pound Recipe
1 1/2 teaspoons	**active dry yeast**	1 teaspoon
1 tablespoon	**dough enhancer (optional)**	2 teaspoons
3/4 cup	**buckwheat flour**	1/2 cup
1 1/2 tablespoons	**dry milk**	1 tablespoon
3 tablespoons	**sugar**	2 tablespoons
1 1/2 teaspoons	**salt**	1 teaspoon
3/4 cup	**barley flour**	1/2 cup
1 1/2 cups + 3 tablespoons	**bread flour**	1 cup + 2 tablespoons
1 1/2 tablespoons	**butter**	1 tablespoon
9 ounces	**warm water**	3/4 cup

NOTE:
For Panasonic/National machines, use 2 teaspoons of yeast for the 1 1/2-pound loaf.

NUTRITIONAL ANALYSIS

	1 1/2-Pound	1-Pound	
Total **Calories**	1766	1227	
Total **Protein**	54	37	grams
Total **Carbohydrates**	325	229	grams
Total **Fat**	25	17	grams
Total **Saturated Fat**	12	8	grams
Total **Cholesterol**	48	32	milligrams
Total **Sodium**	3253	2169	milligrams
Total **Fiber**	15	10	grams
% **Calories from Fat**	13	12	

Grape Nuts Bread

Take one of your favorite breakfast cereals and make bread with it. It comes out with a wonderful nutty taste and great crunchy texture. Have it for breakfast along with your bowl of Grape-Nuts.

INGREDIENTS

1 1/2-Pound Recipe		1-Pound Recipe
1 1/2 teaspoons	**active dry yeast**	1 teaspoon
1 tablespoon	**dough enhancer (optional)**	2 teaspoons
1/2 cup	**Grape-Nuts cereal**	1/4 cup
1 1/2 tablespoons	**dry milk**	1 tablespoon
3 tablespoons	**sugar**	2 tablespoons
1 1/2 teaspoons	**salt**	1 teaspoon
1 1/4 cups	**whole-wheat flour**	3/4 cup
1 1/2 cups	**bread flour**	1 cup
1 1/2 tablespoons	**butter**	1 tablespoon
9 ounces	**warm water**	3/4 cup

NOTE:
For Panasonic/National machines, use 2 teaspoons of yeast for the 1 1/2-pound loaf.

NUTRITIONAL ANALYSIS

	1 1/2-Pound	1-Pound	
Total **Calories**	1800	1130	
Total **Protein**	56	35	grams
Total **Carbohydrates**	345	215	grams
Total **Fat**	24	15	grams
Total **Saturated Fat**	12	8	grams
Total **Cholesterol**	48	32	milligrams
Total **Sodium**	3593	2338	milligrams
Total **Fiber**	28	17	grams
% **Calories from Fat**	12	12	

Sunflower-Nut Bread

This recipe combines sunflower seeds, nuts, whole wheat, and rolled oats, making a tangy-flavored light-textured bread. For extra crunchiness, add the seeds and nuts after the first rise instead of with the rest of the ingredients.

INGREDIENTS

1 1/2-Pound Recipe		1-Pound Recipe
2 tablespoons	**active dry yeast**	1 1/2 teaspoons
2 tablespoons	**sunflower seeds**	4 teaspoons
2 tablespoons	**chopped nuts**	4 teaspoons
1/2 cup	**rolled oats**	1/2 cup
1/2 cup	**whole-wheat flour**	1/2 cup
1 teaspoon	**salt**	1/2 teaspoon
1 tablespoon	**brown sugar**	2 teaspoons
2 cups	**bread flour**	1 1/2 cups
4 teaspoons	**olive oil**	1 tablespoon
1/2 cup	**warm water**	3 ounces
1 1/2 tablespoons	**butter**	1 tablespoon
5 ounces	**warm milk**	3 1/2 ounces

NOTES:

1. For Panasonic/National machines, use 3 1/2 teaspoons of yeast for the 1 1/2-pound loaf.
2. For DAK/Welbilt machines, use 5 ounces of warm water for the 1 1/2-pound loaf.

NUTRITIONAL ANALYSIS

	1 1/2-Pound	1-Pound	
Total **Calories**	1975	1412	
Total **Protein**	60	44	grams
Total **Carbohydrates**	298	215	grams
Total **Fat**	62	44	grams
Total **Saturated Fat**	17	12	grams
Total **Cholesterol**	53	35	milligrams
Total **Sodium**	2225	1131	milligrams
Total **Fiber**	18	15	grams
% Calories from Fat	28	28	

Barley Bread

If you like the sweet taste of barley, you'll enjoy this bread's distinctive barley flavor. It is a light-colored bread, with good texture and a whole-grain taste, punctuated by a light sesame flavor.

INGREDIENTS

1½-Pound Recipe		1-Pound Recipe
1½ tablespoons	**active dry yeast**	1 teaspoon
1 tablespoon	**dough enhancer (optional)**	2 teaspoons
2 teaspoons	**sesame seeds**	1½ teaspoons
1½ tablespoons	**dry milk**	1 tablespoon
3 tablespoons	**sugar**	2 tablespoons
1½ teaspoons	**salt**	1 teaspoon
1 cup	**barley flour**	¾ cup
2 cups	**bread flour**	1¼ cups
1½ tablespoons	**butter**	1 tablespoon
9 ounces	**warm water**	¾ cup

NOTES:

1. For Panasonic/National machines, use 3 teaspoons of yeast for the 1½-pound loaf.
2. For DAK/Welbilt machines, use 10 ounces of warm water for the 1½-pound loaf.

NUTRITIONAL ANALYSIS

	1½-Pound	1-Pound	
Total **Calories**	1754	1173	
Total **Protein**	53	35	grams
Total **Carbohydrates**	312	206	grams
Total **Fat**	27	19	grams
Total **Saturated Fat**	12	8	grams
Total **Cholesterol**	48	32	milligrams
Total **Sodium**	3255	2170	milligrams
Total **Fiber**	19	14	grams
% **Calories from Fat**	14	15	

Buckwheat Bread

This is the bread for buckwheat lovers. Because of its strong buckwheat flavor and texture, it is excellent with vegetable soups or for morning toast.

INGREDIENTS

1½-Pound Recipe		1-Pound Recipe
1½ teaspoons	**active dry yeast**	1 teaspoon
1 tablespoon	**dough enhancer (optional)**	2 teaspoons
1½ tablespoons	**dry milk**	1 tablespoon
2 tablespoons	**sugar**	2 tablespoons
1¾ cups + 2 tablespoons	**bread flour**	1¼ cups
1½ teaspoons	**salt**	1 teaspoon
1 tablespoon	**wheat or oar bran**	2 teaspoons
¼ cup	**wheat germ**	2 tablespoons
1¼ cups	**buckwheat flour**	¾ cup
1½ tablespoons	**butter**	1 tablespoon
9 ounces	**warm water**	¾ cup

NOTES:

1. For Panasonic/National machines, use 3 teaspoons of yeast for the 1½-pound loaf.
2. For DAK/Welbilt machines, use 10 ounces of warm water in the 1½-pound loaf.

NUTRITIONAL ANALYSIS

	1½-Pound	1-Pound	
Total **Calories**	1881	1207	
Total **Protein**	65	41	grams
Total **Carbohydrates**	353	226	grams
Total **Fat**	30	19	grams
Total **Saturated Fat**	13	8	grams
Total **Cholesterol**	48	32	milligrams
Total **Sodium**	3254	2170	milligrams
Total **Fiber**	8	5	grams
% Calories from Fat	14	14	

Oat Bran Bread

In addition to its good flavor, oat bran has been proven to be one of the healthiest of bread ingredients. This bread is a fine addition to any breakfast table.

INGREDIENTS

1 1/2-Pound Recipe		1-Pound Recipe
1 1/2 teaspoons	**active dry yeast**	1 teaspoon
2 tablespoons	**dry milk**	1 1/2 tablespoons
2 tablespoons	**sugar**	2 1/2 tablespoons
1/2 cup	**oat bran**	1/4 cup
1 cup	**oat flour**	3/4 cup
1 1/2 teaspoons	**salt**	1 teaspoon
1 1/2 cups	**bread flour**	1 cup
1 1/2 tablespoons	**butter**	1 tablespoon
9 ounces	**warm water**	3/4 cup

NOTES:

1. For Panasonic/National machines, use 3 teaspoons of yeast for the 1 1/2-pound loaf.
2. For DAK/Welbilt machines, use 10 ounces of warm water for the 1 1/2-pound loaf.

NUTRITIONAL ANALYSIS

	1 1/2-Pound	1-Pound	
Total **Calories**	1666	1117	
Total **Protein**	53	35	grams
Total **Carbohydrates**	315	211	grams
Total **Fat**	26	17	grams
Total **Saturated Fat**	11	8	grams
Total **Cholesterol**	49	33	milligrams
Total **Sodium**	3270	2185	milligrams
Total **Fiber**	27	18	grams
% **Calories from Fat**	14	14	

Multigrain Bread

This bread combines five types of whole-grain flours for a grain lover's delight. All of these grains together create a unique loaf with a distinctive, but elusive flavor.

INGREDIENTS

1½-Pound Recipe		1-Pound Recipe
3 teaspoons	**active dry yeast**	2 teaspoons
1 tablespoon	**dough enhancer (optional)**	2 teaspoons
1½ teaspoons	**gluten**	1 teaspoon
¼ cup	**buckwheat flour**	2 tablespoons
¼ cup	**whole-wheat flour**	2 tablespoons
2 cups	**bread flour**	1½ cups
¼ cup	**oat flour**	2 tablespoons
¼ cup	**barley flour**	2 tablespoons
3 tablespoons	**oat bran**	2 tablespoons
2 tablespoons	**wheat germ**	4 teaspoons
1 teaspoon	**salt**	½ teaspoon
1 tablespoon	**brown sugar**	2 teaspoons
2 tablespoons	**butter**	1½ tablespoons
9 ounces	**warm water**	¾ cup

NOTES:

1. For Panasonic/National machines, use 3½ teaspoons of yeast for the 1½-pound loaf.
2. For DAK/Welbilt machines, use 10 ounces of warm water in the 1½-pound loaf.

NUTRITIONAL ANALYSIS

	1½-Pound	1-Pound	
Total **Calories**	1772	1227	
Total **Protein**	61	42	grams
Total **Carbohydrates**	313	214	grams
Total **Fat**	33	24	grams
Total **Saturated Fat**	15	11	grams
Total **Cholesterol**	62	47	milligrams
Total **Sodium**	2149	1078	milligrams
Total **Fiber**	20	12	grams
% Calories from Fat	17	18	

Barley Three-Seed Bread

The combination of barley, poppy seeds, sesame seeds, and sunflower seeds makes this bread unique, both in flavor and texture. It's excellent with salads.

INGREDIENTS

1$^1/_2$-Pound Recipe		1-Pound Recipe
1$^1/_2$ teaspoons	**active dry yeast**	1 teaspoon
3 tablespoons	**sugar**	2 tablespoons
2 cups	**bread flour**	1$^1/_2$ cups
1 teaspoon	**poppy seeds**	$^1/_2$ teaspoon
2 teaspoons	**sunflower seeds**	1$^1/_2$ teaspoons
2 teaspoons	**sesame seeds**	1$^1/_2$ teaspoons
1 tablespoon	**dough enhancer (optional)**	$^1/_2$ tablespoon
1 cup	**barley flour**	$^2/_3$ cup
$^1/_2$ teaspoon	**garlic salt**	$^1/_4$ teaspoon
1 teaspoon	**salt**	$^1/_2$ teaspoon
1 tablespoon	**nonfat dry milk**	$^1/_2$ tablespoon
1 cup + 1 tablespoon	**warm water**	5$^1/_2$ ounces
1$^1/_2$ tablespoons	**butter**	1 tablespoon

NOTES:

1. For machines with yeast dispensers, use 3 teaspoons of yeast for the 1$^1/_2$-pound loaf.
2. This bread is somewhat crumbly. The addition of the dough enhancer, if available, will help the bread stick together, and give it a smoother texture.

NUTRITIONAL ANALYSIS

	1$^1/_2$-Pound	1-Pound	
Total **Calories**	1790	1192	
Total **Protein**	53	35	grams
Total **Carbohydrates**	312	208	grams
Total **Fat**	31	21	grams
Total **Saturated Fat**	12	8	grams
Total **Cholesterol**	48	32	milligrams
Total **Sodium**	3240	1622	milligrams
Total **Fiber**	20	13	grams
% **Calories from Fat**	16	16	

Brown Rice Bread

A soft, moist texture and light brown color characterize this bread. White rice can be substituted for brown rice.

INGREDIENTS

$1^1/_2$-Pound Recipe		1-Pound Recipe
$1^1/_2$ teaspoons	**active dry yeast**	1 teaspoon
1 teaspoon	**sugar**	$^1/_2$ teaspoon
3 cups	**bread flour**	2 cups
$1^1/_2$ teaspoons	**salt**	1 teaspoon
$^3/_4$ cup	**brown rice (ccoked)**	$^1/_2$ cup
$1^1/_2$ tablespoons	**olive**	1 tablespoon
3 tablespoons	**honey**	2 tablespoons
$4^1/_2$ ounces	**warm buttermilk**	3 ounces
3 ounces	**warm water**	$^1/_4$ cup

NOTE:
For machines with yeast dispensers, use 3 teaspoons of yeast for the $1^1/_2$-pound loaf.

NUTRITIONAL ANALYSIS

	$1^1/_2$-Pound	1-Pound	
Total **Calories**	2098	1396	
Total **Protein**	60	40	grams
Total **Carbohydrates**	394	262	grams
Total **Fat**	29	20	grams
Total **Saturated Fat**	4	3	grams
Total **Cholesterol**	12	8	milligrams
Total **Sodium**	3295	2197	milligrams
Total **Fiber**	7	5	grams
% Calories from Fat	13	13	

Millet Bread

Millet is a small, round, hard grain that requires soaking before use. It is also available in ground form as millet flour. The texture of this bread is crunchy, though also light due to the mixture of whole-wheat and bread flours.

INGREDIENTS

1 1/2-Pound Recipe		1-Pound Recipe
1 1/2 teaspoons	**active dry yeast**	1 teaspoon
1 cup	**whole-wheat flour**	2/3 cup
2 cups	**bread flour**	1 1/2 cups
1 teaspoon	**salt**	1/2 teaspoon
1 cup	**warm water**	2/3 cup
1/2 cup	**raw millet (or millet cereal)**	1/3 cup
2 tablespoons	**olive oil**	1 1/2 tablespoons
3 tablespoons	**honey**	2 tablespoons
1	**egg**	1

NOTES:

1. For machines with yeast dispensers, use 3 teaspoons of yeast for the 1 1/2-pound loaf.
2. Soak the millet in the warm water for 45-60 minutes before adding the grain and the water to the recipe.

NUTRITIONAL ANALYSIS

	1 1/2-Pound	1-Pound	
Total **Calories**	2279	1645	
Total **Protein**	68	50	grams
Total **Carbohydrates**	409	289	grams
Total **Fat**	43	33	grams
Total **Saturated Fat**	7	5	grams
Total **Cholesterol**	213	213	milligrams
Total **Sodium**	2207	1137	milligrams
Total **Fiber**	21	14	grams
% **Calories from Fat**	17	18	

Sesame Quinoa Bread

Quinoa, native to South America, is one of the grains highest in protein. Since it contains no gluten, it must be combined with wheat flour. Sesame Quinoa Bread has a nutty, earthy flavor, making it an excellent sandwich bread.

INGREDIENTS

1½-Pound Recipe		1-Pound Recipe
1½ teaspoons	**active dry yeast**	1 teaspoon
3 tablespoons	**sugar**	2 tablespoons
2 cups	**bread flour**	1⅓ cups
½ cup	**quinoa flour**	⅓ cup
3 tablespoons	**sesame seeds**	2 tablespoons
½ teaspoon	**oregano**	¼ teaspoon
½ teaspoon	**ground caraway seeds**	¼ teaspoon
½ cup	**whole-wheat flour**	⅓ cup
1½ teaspoons	**salt**	1 teaspoon
1½ tablespoons	**nonfat dry milk**	⅔ cup
9 ounces	**warm water**	¾ cup
2 tablespoons	**butter**	1½ tablespoons

NOTE:
For machines with yeast dispensers, use 3 teaspoons of yeast for the 1½-pound loaf.

NUTRITIONAL ANALYSIS

	1½-Pound	1-Pound	
Total **Calories**	2053	1379	
Total **Protein**	62	41	grams
Total **Carbohydrates**	350	232	grams
Total **Fat**	47	33	grams
Total **Saturated Fat**	17	13	grams
Total **Cholesterol**	64	48	milligrams
Total **Sodium**	3256	2171	milligrams
Total **Fiber**	14	9	grams
% Calories from Fat	21	22	

Soy Bread

This white bread is enriched by the addition of high-protein soy flour.

INGREDIENTS

1 1/2-Pound Recipe		1-Pound Recipe
1 1/2 teaspoons	**active dry yeast**	1 teaspoon
1 1/2 tablespoons	**sugar**	1 tablespoon
1/2 cup	**soy flour**	1/3 cup
2 1/2 cups	**bread flour**	1 2/3 cups
1 1/2 teaspoons	**salt**	1 teaspoon
9 ounces	**warm milk**	3/4 cup
1 1/2 tablespoons	**butter**	1 tablespoon

NOTE:
For machines with yeast dispensers, use 3 teaspoons of yeast for the 1 1/2-pound loaf.

NUTRITIONAL ANALYSIS

	1 1/2-Pound	1-Pound	
Total **Calories**	1746	1165	
Total **Protein**	75	50	grams
Total **Carbohydrates**	300	200	grams
Total **Fat**	27	18	grams
Total **Saturated Fat**	13	9	grams
Total **Cholesterol**	58	39	milligrams
Total **Sodium**	3355	2236	milligrams
Total **Fiber**	8	5	grams
% **Calories from Fat**	14	14	

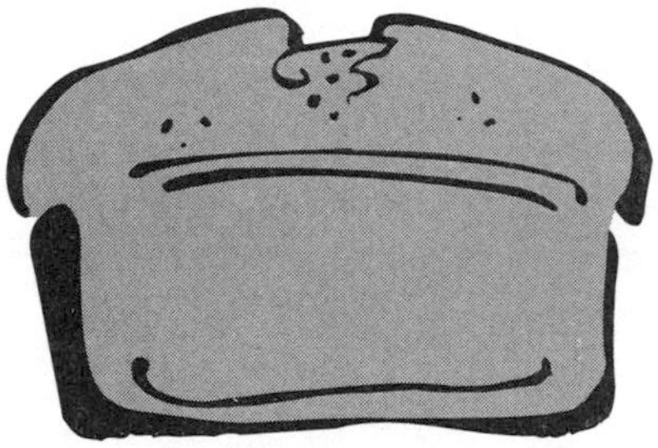

MULTIPLE-GRAIN BREADS

This section features seven mixed-grain breads in which the taste of grain dominates. These unique combinations of grains are especially designed for whole-grain bread lovers.

Bran & Rye Bread

This light wheat-rye bread has added oat bran for texture, flavor, and nutrients. It has a light wheat taste and texture.

INGREDIENTS

1½-Pound Recipe		1-Pound Recipe
1½ teaspoons	**active dry yeast**	1 teaspoon
2½ tablespoons	**brown sugar**	1½ tablespoons
1 cup + 1½ tablespoons	**bread flour**	⅔ cup + 1 tablespoon
½ cup	**whole-wheat flour**	⅓ cup
¾ cup	**rye flour**	½ cup
¾ cup	**oat bran**	½ cup
2 teaspoons	**salt**	1½ teaspoons
2 tablespoons	**butter**	1½ tablespoons
9 ounces	**warm buttermilk**	¾ cup

NOTES:

1. For machines with yeast dispensers, use 3 teaspoons of yeast for the 1½-pound loaf.
2. If your machine is equipped with a whole-grain cycle, use it for this bread.

NUTRITIONAL ANALYSIS

	1½-Pound	1-Pound	
Total **Calories**	1691	1130	
Total **Protein**	60	40	grams
Total **Carbohydrates**	300	197	grams
Total **Fat**	35	25	grams
Total **Saturated Fat**	17	12	grams
Total **Cholesterol**	85	62	milligrams
Total **Sodium**	4460	3328	milligrams
Total **Fiber**	31	21	grams
% **Calories from Fat**	18	20	

Corn, Wheat, & Rye Bread

This is a very crunchy whole-grain bread with a good wheat flavor and a hint of rye.

INGREDIENTS

1 1/2-Pound Recipe		1-Pound Recipe
2 teaspoons	**active dry yeast**	1 1/2 teaspoons
3 tablespoons	**brown sugar**	2 tablespoons
1/2 cup	**cornmeal**	1/4 cup + 2 tablespoons
1 1/4 cups	**whole-wheat flour**	1 cup
1 1/4 cups	**rye flour**	3/4 cup
1 1/2 teaspoons	**salt**	1 teaspoon
3 tablespoons	**butter**	2 tablespoons
9 ounces	**warm water**	3/4 cup

NOTES:

1. For machines with yeast dispensers, use 3 teaspoons of yeast for the 1 1/2-pound loaf.
2. If your machine is equipped with a whole-grain cycle, use it for this bread.

NUTRITIONAL ANALYSIS

	1 1/2-Pound	1-Pound	
Total **Calories**	1648	1158	
Total **Protein**	40	29	grams
Total **Carbohydrates**	296	210	grams
Total **Fat**	42	28	grams
Total **Saturated Fat**	22	15	grams
Total **Cholesterol**	93	62	milligrams
Total **Sodium**	3242	2164	milligrams
Total **Fiber**	45	32	grams
% **Calories from Fat**	23	22	

Mixed-Grain Bread

This bread combines many different grains for a full-grain taste. It doesn't rise much, due to the low-gluten content of the ingredients, but it is a wonderful, healthful bread with an earthy aroma.

INGREDIENTS

1½-Pound Recipe		1-Pound Recipe
2½ teaspoons	**active dry yeast**	1½ teaspoons
⅔ cup	**bread flour**	½ cup
½ teaspoon	**caraway seeds**	½ teaspoon
2 teaspoons	**salt**	1½ teaspoons
½ cup	**rice flour**	⅓ cup
⅔ cup	**buckwheat flour**	½ cup
⅔ cup	**oat flour**	½ cup
⅔ cup	**rye flour**	½ cup
5 tablespoons	**molasses**	4 tablespoons
1	**egg**	1
7 ounces	**warm water**	4½ ounces
3 tablespoons	**raisins**	2 tablespoons
2 tablespoons	**gluten powder (optional)**	1½ tablespoons

NOTES:

1. For machines with yeast dispensers, use 4½ teaspoons of yeast for the 1½-pound loaf.
2. If your machine is equipped with a whole-grain cycle, use it for this bread.
3. Raisins may be added at the mix-cycle beep, if your machine is so equipped.

NUTRITIONAL ANALYSIS

	1½-Pound	1-Pound	
Total **Calories**	1877	1403	
Total **Protein**	52	39	grams
Total **Carbohydrates**	392	289	grams
Total **Fat**	13	11	grams
Total **Saturated Fat**	3	2	grams
Total **Cholesterol**	213	213	milligrams
Total **Sodium**	4414	3329	milligrams
Total **Fiber**	27	20	grams
% **Calories from Fat**	6	7	

Oat, Rice, & Rye Bread

This bread doesn't rise much, but with its tight texture and flat top, it tastes delicious.

INGREDIENTS

1½-Pound Recipe		1-Pound Recipe
2 teaspoons	**active dry yeast**	1½ teaspoons
1½ tablespoons	**gluten powder**	1 tablespoon
¾ cup	**bread flour**	½ cup
1 teaspoon	**ground caraway seeds**	½ teaspoon
¾ cup	**rice flour**	½ cup
¾ cup	**oat flour**	½ cup
¾ cup	**rye flour**	½ cup
1½ teaspoons	**salt**	1 teaspoon
2 tablespoons	**brown sugar**	1½ tablespoons
2 tablespoons	**butter**	1½ tablespoons
9 ounces	**warm water**	¾ cup

NOTES:

1. For machines with yeast dispensers, use 4 teaspoons of yeast for the 1½-pound loaf.
2. If your machine is equipped with a whole-grain cycle, use it for this bread.
3. For a slightly higher rise, try adding an extra 1 teaspoon of yeast.

NUTRITIONAL ANALYSIS

	1½-Pound	1-Pound	
Total **Calories**	1774	1208	
Total **Protein**	51	34	grams
Total **Carbohydrates**	330	222	grams
Total **Fat**	30	22	grams
Total **Saturated Fat**	15	11	grams
Total **Cholesterol**	62	47	milligrams
Total **Sodium**	3217	2146	milligrams
Total **Fiber**	30	20	grams
% Calories from Fat	15	16	

Whole-Wheat & Rice Bread

This bread uses only wheat and rice flours, so the result is a bread similar to 100 percent-wheat bread, both in texture and flavor. The rice flour has a smoothing effect on the texture, but it contains no gluten, so the loaf will rise slightly less than a normal 100 percent-wheat loaf.

INGREDIENTS

1 1/2-Pound Recipe		1-Pound Recipe
2 teaspoons	**active dry yeast**	1 1/2 teaspoons
2 1/4 cups	**whole-wheat flour**	1 1/2 cups
1/2 teaspoon	**mace**	1/4 teaspoon
3/4 cup	**rice flour**	1/2 cup
2 teaspoons	**salt**	1 1/2 teaspoons
2 tablespoons	**butter**	1 1/2 tablespoons
3 tablespoons	**honey**	2 tablespoons
1 cup	**warm water**	5 1/2 ounces
1/4 cup	**raisins**	3 tablespoons

NOTES:

1. For machines with yeast dispensers, use 4 teaspoons of yeast for the 1 1/2-pound loaf.
2. If your machine is equipped with a whole-grain cycle, use it for this bread.
3. Raisins may be added at the mix-cycle beep, if your machine is so equiped.
4. For machines with low power motors, add 2 tablespoons of warm water for the 1 1/2-pound loaf.

NUTRITIONAL ANALYSIS

	1 1/2-Pound	1-Pound	
Total **Calories**	1852	1289	
Total **Protein**	47	32	grams
Total **Carbohydrates**	369	256	grams
Total **Fat**	30	22	grams
Total **Saturated Fat**	16	12	grams
Total **Cholesterol**	62	47	milligrams
Total **Sodium**	4276	3208	milligrams
Total **Fiber**	40	27	grams
% **Calories from Fat**	14	15	

Whole-Wheat, Bran, & Oat Bread

This bread has a soft texture and a mild wheat-oat flavor. Because bread flour comprises half the flour, it rises well and yields a nice-looking, good-tasting loaf.

INGREDIENTS

1½-Pound Recipe		1-Pound Recipe
2 teaspoons	**active dry yeast**	1½ teaspoons
3 tablespoons	**brown sugar**	2 tablespoons
1½ tablespoons	**gluten powder**	1 tablespoon
1½ cups	**bread flour**	1 cup
⅓ cup	**oat bran**	¼ cup
¾ cup	**oat flour**	½ cup
¾ cup	**whole-wheat flour**	½ cup
2 teaspoons	**salt**	1½ teaspoons
3½ tablespoons	**butter**	2½ tablespoons
1¼ cups	**warm water**	6½ ounces

NOTE:
For machines with yeast dispensers, use 3½ teaspoons of yeast for the 1½-pound loaf.

NUTRITIONAL ANALYSIS

	1½-Pound	1-Pound	
Total **Calories**	2031	1406	
Total **Protein**	67	45	grams
Total **Carbohydrates**	344	238	grams
Total **Fat**	50	35	grams
Total **Saturated Fat**	26	18	grams
Total **Cholesterol**	109	78	milligrams
Total **Sodium**	4289	3217	milligrams
Total **Fiber**	32	22	grams
% **Calories from Fat**	22	22	

Whole-Wheat, Rye, & Oat Bread

A good dense texture and hearty flavor characterize this bread. It's excellent eaten warm or toasted, and it's especially good with all kinds of cheese.

INGREDIENTS

1½-Pound Recipe		1-Pound Recipe
2 teaspoons	**active dry yeast**	1½ teaspoons
¾ cup	**oat flour**	½ cup
¾ cup	**rye flour**	½ cup
1½ cups	**whole-wheat flour**	1 cup
1½ teaspoons	**salt**	1 teaspoon
3 tablespoons	**butter**	2 tablespoons
3 tablespoons	**honey**	2 tablespoons
1 cup +1 tablespoon	**warm water**	5½ ounces

NOTES:

1. For machines with yeast dispensers, use 4 teaspoons of yeast for the 1½-pound loaf.
2. If your machine is equipped with a whole-grain cycle, use it for this bread.

NUTRITIONAL ANALYSIS

	1½-Pound	1-Pound	
Total **Calories**	1675	1118	
Total **Protein**	45	30	grams
Total **Carbohydrates**	304	203	grams
Total **Fat**	41	27	grams
Total **Saturated Fat**	22	15	grams
Total **Cholesterol**	93	62	milligrams
Total **Sodium**	3209	2139	milligrams
Total **Fiber**	47	31	grams
% Calories from Fat	22	22	

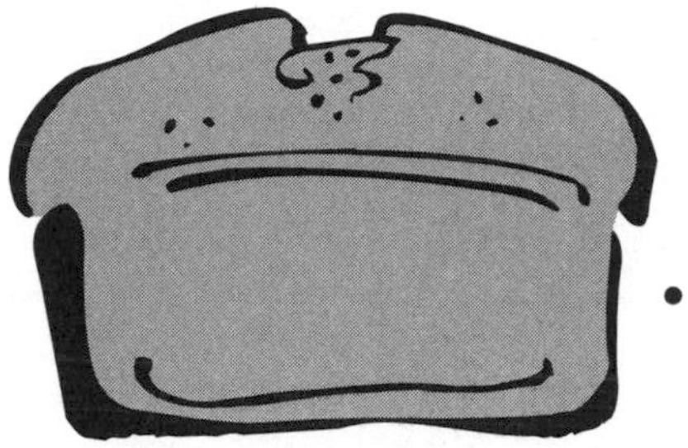

SPICE & SWEET BREADS

If you like a lot of different flavors in your breads, these recipes will appeal to you. The spice breads use many different types of spices and seasonings to give them unique flavors. The sweet breads combine natural sweeteners with other bread ingredients to give you bread that will satisfy your sweet tooth in a low-calorie and natural way.

Cumin Spice Bread

Cumin, a relative of oregano, is a common spice in most Mexican foods. This bread has a distinct cumin flavor while still possessing the wonderful texture and taste of whole-grain flours.

INGREDIENTS

1 1/2-Pound Recipe		1-Pound Recipe
3 teaspoons	**active dry yeast**	2 teaspoons
2 teaspoons	**dried orange peel**	1 1/2 teaspoons
1 teaspoon	**sugar**	1 teaspoon
2 teaspoons	**cumin powder**	1 1/2 teaspoons
1/2 cup	**rye flour**	1/3 cup
1 teaspoon	**salt**	1/2 teaspoon
1/2 cup	**whole-wheat flour**	1/2 cup
2 cups	**bread flour**	1 1/4 cups
7 ounces	**warm milk**	6 ounces
5 tablespoons	**honey**	3 tablespoons+ 1 teaspoon
3 tablespoons	**olive oil**	2 tablespoons

NUTRITIONAL ANALYSIS

	1 1/2-Pound	1-Pound	
Total **Calories**	2200	1583	
Total **Protein**	61	46	grams
Total **Carbohydrates**	385	281	grams
Total **Fat**	51	35	grams
Total **Saturated Fat**	8	6	grams
Total **Cholesterol**	9	8	milligrams
Total **Sodium**	2257	1170	milligrams
Total **Fiber**	14	12	grams
% **Calories from Fat**	21	20	

Carrot Bread

• • •

see page 150

Sweet-Potato Bread

• • •

see page 151

Sourdough French Bread

• • •

see page 157

Grumbera Bread

• • •

see page 176

Indian Bread

• • •

see page 177

Ethiopian Spice Bread

• • •

see page 215

Panettone

• • •

see page 214

Chive & Garlic Bread

• • •

see page 216

Crescia al Formaggio

• • •

see page 217

Weissbrot mit Kummel

• • •

see page 218

Danish Sour Bread

• • •

see page 219

Italian Herb Bread

• • •

see page 220

Dilly Bread

This is an old family favorite. The cottage cheese (I use low-fat) gives it a great texture and flavor that is perfect with a salad. Note that all-purpose flour is used to maintain the original texture.

INGREDIENTS

1½-Pound Recipe		1-Pound Recipe
2½ teaspoons	**active dry yeast**	1½ teaspoons
3 cups	**all-purpose flour**	2 cups
½ teaspoon	**baking soda**	¼ teaspoon
1½ teaspoons	**salt**	1 teaspoon
1½ tablespoons	**dill weed**	1 tablespoon
2½ tablespoons	**sugar**	1½ tablespoons
2 tablespoons	**warm water**	1 tablespoon
3	**eggs**	2
1 cup	**cottage cheese**	¾ cup

NOTE:
For Panasonic/National machines, use 3½ teaspoons of yeast for the 1½-pound loaf.

NUTRITIONAL ANALYSIS

	1½-Pound	1-Pound	
Total **Calories**	2056	1379	
Total **Protein**	100	69	grams
Total **Carbohydrates**	343	227	grams
Total **Fat**	26	18	grams
Total **Saturated Fat**	8	5	grams
Total **Cholesterol**	669	449	milligrams
Total **Sodium**	4425	3035	milligrams
Total **Fiber**	7	5	grams
% **Calories from Fat**	11	12	

Peppy Cheese Bread

This bread has a snappy cheese flavor and is great for a ham or tuna sandwich. Cut it into small pieces for tasty and attractive sandwiches.

INGREDIENTS

1 1/2-Pound Recipe		1-Pound Recipe
1 1/2 teaspoons	**active dry yeast**	1 teaspoon
3 cups	**bread flour**	2 cups
3 tablespoons	**Parmesan cheese**	2 tablespoons
1/4 cup	**grated Swiss cheese**	2 tablespoons
1 1/2 teaspoons	**oregano**	1 teaspoon
1/4 cup	**grated cheddar cheese**	2 tablespoons
3 tablespoons	**wheat germ**	2 tablespoons
4 teaspoons	**sugar**	1 tablespoon
1 1/2 teaspoons	**Louisiana-style hot sauce**	1 teaspoon
2 1/2 tablespoons	**butter**	1 1/2 tablespoons
9 ounces	**warm water**	3/4 cup

NOTES:

1. For Panasonic/National machines, use 2 1/2 teaspoons of yeast for the 1 1/2-pound loaf.
2. Because of the fresh cheese content, use a lighter crust setting.
3. Because of the wetter dough caused by the melting cheese, the top of the loaf may fall during baking. This will not affect the taste of the bread.
4. The fresh cheeses may be added at the mix cycle, if desired.

NUTRITIONAL ANALYSIS

	1 1/2-Pound	1-Pound	
Total **Calories**	2162	1395	
Total **Protein**	77	49	grams
Total **Carbohydrates**	329	221	grams
Total **Fat**	60	35	grams
Total **Saturated Fat**	33	19	grams
Total **Cholesterol**	144	82	milligrams
Total **Sodium**	747	444	milligrams
Total **Fiber**	9	6	grams
% **Calories from Fat**	25	23	

Taco Bread

The cornmeal and taco seasoning in this bread actually give it the flavor of a taco. It goes great with hot Southwestern chili.

INGREDIENTS

1½-Pound Recipe		1-Pound Recipe
1½ teaspoons	**active dry yeast**	1 teaspoon
2 cups	**bread flour**	1¼ cups
3 tablespoons	**taco seasoning**	2 tablespoons
¼ cup	**whole-wheat flour**	2 tablespoons
¾ cup	**cornmeal**	½ cup
1 teaspoon	**garlic salt**	½ teaspoon
3 tablespoons	**taco seasoning**	2 tablespoons
2 tablespoons	**sugar**	4 teaspoons
1½ tablespoons	**olive oil**	1 tablespoon
9 ounces	**warm water**	¾ cup

NOTE:
For Panasonic/National machines, use 2½ teaspoons of yeast for the 1½-pound loaf.

NUTRITIONAL ANALYSIS

	1½-Pound	1-Pound	
Total **Calories**	1803	1254	
Total **Protein**	47	32	grams
Total **Carbohydrates**	337	236	grams
Total **Fat**	30	21	grams
Total **Saturated Fat**	4	3	grams
Total **Cholesterol**	0	0	milligrams
Total **Sodium**	5740	3482	milligrams
Total **Fiber**	18	15	grams
% **Calories from Fat**	15	15	

Cheddar-Parmesan Bread

Watch out here! This is a rich bread (due to the cheese content), and no butter is needed. Just pop this bread right in your mouth. It is an excellent bread for a ham sandwich (no cheese needed), and the flavor will remind you of Cheese-It crackers.

INGREDIENTS

1 1/2-Pound Recipe		1-Pound Recipe
2 teaspoons	**active dry yeast**	1 1/2 teaspoons
2 1/2 cups	**bread flour**	1 3/4 cups
2 1/2 tablespoons	**dried minced onion**	5 teaspoons
1 1/4 cups	**grated cheddar cheese**	3/4 cup
1 1/2 teaspoons	**paprika**	1 teaspoon
2 1/2 tablespoons	**Parmesan cheese**	5 teaspoons
1 teaspoon	**dry mustard**	1/2 teaspoon
1/2 teaspoon	**salt**	1/2 teaspoon
3 1/2 teaspoons	**sugar**	1 1/2 teaspoons
2 1/2 tablespoons	**butter**	5 teaspoons
7 ounces	**warm milk**	4 1/2 ounces

NOTES:

1. For Panasonic/National machines, use 3 teaspoons of yeast for the 1 1/2-pound loaf.
2. Use a light-crust setting, because the cheese content of this bread gives it a tendency to bake to a dark-brown crust.

NUTRITIONAL ANALYSIS

	1 1/2-Pound	1-Pound	
Total **Calories**	2329	1556	
Total **Protein**	93	61	grams
Total **Carbohydrates**	289	202	grams
Total **Fat**	89	56	grams
Total **Saturated Fat**	52	33	grams
Total **Cholesterol**	245	153	milligrams
Total **Sodium**	2296	1826	milligrams
Total **Fiber**	7	5	grams
% **Calories from Fat**	34	32	

Herb Bread

If you like herbs and spices, you will love this bread. It combines small amounts of herbs for just the right flavor. If you have any left over, dry it, and use it for turkey stuffing.

INGREDIENTS

1½-Pound Recipe		1-Pound Recipe
1 teaspoon	**active dry yeast**	½ teaspoon
2 tablespoons	**sugar**	4 teaspoons
3 cups	**bread flour**	2 cups
2 teaspoons	**celery**	1½ teaspoons
1 teaspoon	**ground sage**	½ teaspoon
½ teaspoon	**nutmeg**	¼ teaspoon
1½ teaspoons	**salt**	1 teaspoon
1 teaspoon	**parsley**	½ teaspoon
1	**egg**	1
¾ cup	**warm milk**	½ cup
2 tablespoons	**butter**	1½ tablespoons
2 ounces	**warm water**	3 tablespoons

NOTES:

1. For Panasonic/National machines, use 2 teaspoons of yeast for the 1½-pound loaf.
2. For DAK/Welbilt machines, use 3 ounces of warm water for the 1½-pound loaf.

NUTRITIONAL ANALYSIS

	1½-Pound	1-Pound	
Total **Calories**	1960	1347	
Total **Protein**	64	44	grams
Total **Carbohydrates**	335	223	grams
Total **Fat**	38	29	grams
Total **Saturated Fat**	19	14	grams
Total **Cholesterol**	283	265	milligrams
Total **Sodium**	3369	2267	milligrams
Total **Fiber**	7	5	grams
% **Calories from Fat**	18	19	

Pumpkin Pie Bread

My kids eat this bread before it has a chance to cool off. It tastes like pumpkin pie and makes a great after-school treat.

INGREDIENTS

1½-Pound Recipe		1-Pound Recipe
2 teaspoons	**active dry yeast**	1½ teaspoons
9 tablespoons	**sugar**	6 tablespoons
½ teaspoon	**ginger**	¼ teaspoon
1 teaspoon	**cinnamon**	½ teaspoon
½ teaspoon	**dried lemon peel**	¼ teaspoon
¾ cup	**whole-wheat flour**	½ cup
1 teaspoon	**salt**	½ teaspoon
2½ cups	**bread flour**	1½ cups
¼ cup + 2 tablespoons	**canned pumpkin**	¼ cup
3 ounces	**orange juice**	¼ cup
3 ounces	**warm water**	¼ cup
2	**eggs**	1
1½ tablespoons	**butter**	1 tablespoon

NOTES:

1. For Panasonic/National machines, use 3½ teaspoons of yeast for the 1½-pound loaf.
2. For DAK/Welbilt machines, use ½ cup of warm water in the 1½-pound loaf.

NUTRITIONAL ANALYSIS

	1½-Pound	1-Pound	
Total **Calories**	2225	1458	
Total **Protein**	66	42	grams
Total **Carbohydrates**	419	279	grams
Total **Fat**	35	21	grams
Total **Saturated Fat**	15	9	grams
Total **Cholesterol**	473	244	milligrams
Total **Sodium**	2269	1136	milligrams
Total **Fiber**	17	11	grams
% **Calories from Fat**	14	13	

Hawaiian Bread

This bread works well when you want a sweet substitute for white bread. It's great with jelly or jam.

INGREDIENTS

1½-Pound Recipe		1-Pound Recipe
1½ teaspoons	**active dry yeast**	1 teaspoon
5 tablespoons	**sugar**	3 teaspoons
3 cups	**bread flour**	2 cups
½ teaspoon	**salt**	½ teaspoon
2 tablespoons	**dry milk**	4 teaspoons
2 tablespoons	**instant-mashed potato flakes**	4 teaspoons
¼ teaspoon	**lemon extract**	¼ teaspoon
¼ teaspoon	**vanilla extract**	¼ teaspoon
2	**eggs**	1
4 tablespoons	**butter**	2½ tablespoons
1 cup	**warm water**	5 ounces

NOTE:
For Panasonic/National machines, use 3 teaspoons of yeast for the 1½-pound loaf.

NUTRITIONAL ANALYSIS

	1½-Pound	1-Pound	
Total **Calories**	2351	1511	
Total **Protein**	68	44	grams
Total **Carbohydrates**	371	243	grams
Total **Fat**	64	39	grams
Total **Saturated Fat**	33	20	grams
Total **Cholesterol**	552	292	milligrams
Total **Sodium**	1356	1238	milligrams
Total **Fiber**	7	4	grams
% **Calories from Fat**	25	23	

Peanut Butter & Jelly Bread

This is a fun bread. You can vary it by adding different types of jelly or jam each time you make it.

INGREDIENTS

1½-Pound Recipe		1-Pound Recipe
2 teaspoons	**active dry yeast**	1½ teaspoons
3½ tablespoons	**peanut butter**	2½ tablespoons
3 tablespoons	**jelly or jam**	2 tablespoons
2½ cups	**bread flour**	1½ cups
1½ teaspoons	**salt**	1 teaspoon
2 tablespoons	**sugar**	3½ teaspoons
½ cup	**warm milk**	¼ cup
½ cup	**warm water**	2½ ounces

NOTE:
For Panasonic/National machines, use 3½ teaspoons of yeast for the 1½-pound loaf.

NUTRITIONAL ANALYSIS

	1½-Pound	1-Pound	
Total **Calories**	1886	1175	
Total **Protein**	60	38	grams
Total **Carbohydrates**	333	203	grams
Total **Fat**	35	24	grams
Total **Saturated Fat**	7	5	grams
Total **Cholesterol**	5	3	milligrams
Total **Sodium**	3289	2183	milligrams
Total **Fiber**	10	6	grams
% Calories from Fat	17	19	

Apple Pie Bread

This is so much like the real thing that it even contains apple-pie filling. It is moist, tangy, and a great breakfast bread.

INGREDIENTS

1½-Pound Recipe		1-Pound Recipe
1½ teaspoon	**active dry yeast**	1 teaspoon
1½ teaspoon	**cinnamon**	1 teaspoon
5 tablespoons	**sugar**	3½ tablespoons
3¼ cups + 2 tablespoons	**bread flour**	2¼ cups
1½ teaspoons	**salt**	1 teaspoon
3 tablespoons	**buttermilk powder or dry milk**	4 teaspoons
¾ cup	**apple-pie filling**	½ cup
1½ tablespoons	**butter**	1 tablespoon
4½ ounces	**apple juice**	3 ounces

NOTE:
For Panasonic/National machines, use 3 teaspoons of yeast for the 1½-pound loaf.

NUTRITIONAL ANALYSIS

	1½-Pound	1-Pound	
Total **Calories**	2376	1591	
Total **Protein**	62	42	grams
Total **Carbohydrates**	468	314	grams
Total **Fat**	26	17	grams
Total **Saturated Fat**	12	8	grams
Total **Cholesterol**	57	38	milligrams
Total **Sodium**	3382	2255	milligrams
Total **Fiber**	9	6	grams
% **Calories from Fat**	10	10	

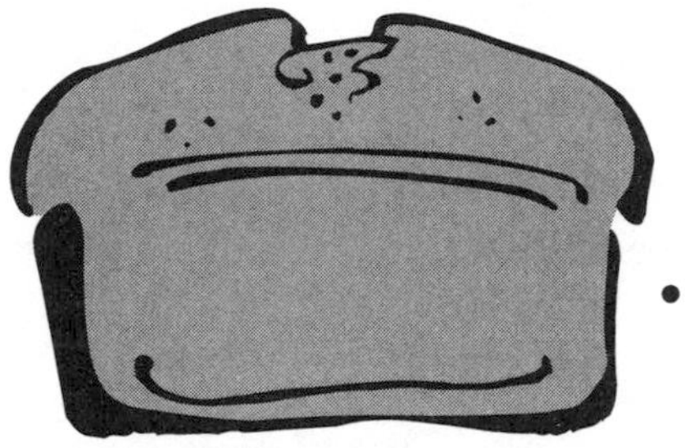

FRUIT & VEGETABLE BREADS

These recipes focus on the variety of flavors available using fruits and vegetables in breads. They vary greatly in their content and texture, but you will find that they all contain natural, nutritious ingredients that are sure to please your palate.

Cinnamon-Raisin Nut Bread

Although not an extremely sweet bread, it is very flavorful. The nuts give it a great crunch, especially if added during the mix cycle.

INGREDIENTS

1½-Pound Recipe		1-Pound Recipe
2 teaspoons	**active dry yeast**	1½ teaspoons
3½ tablespoons	**sugar**	2½ tablespoons
2 cups	**bread flour**	1½ cups
2 teaspoons	**dry milk**	1½ teaspoons
1½ teaspoons	**cinnamon**	1 teaspoon
1 teaspoon	**salt**	½ teaspoon
2½ tablespoons	**honey**	1½ tablespoons
2 tablespoons	**butter**	1½ tablespoons
1	**egg**	1
3 tablespoons	**warm water**	2 tablespoons
3 ounces	**warm milk**	2½ ounces
½ cup	**raisins**	¼ cup
½ cup	**chopped nuts**	¼ cup

NOTES:

1. For Panasonic/National machines, use 3½ teaspoons of yeast for the 1½-pound loaf.
2. For DAK/Welbilt machines, use 5 tablespoons of warm water for the 1½-pound loaf.
3. For best results, add the raisins and chopped nuts after the first mixing. If your machine has a mix cycle, use it and add the raisins and nuts at the "mix" beep.

NUTRITIONAL ANALYSIS

	1½-Pound	1-Pound	
Total **Calories**	2253	1532	
Total **Protein**	57	42	grams
Total **Carbohydrates**	360	248	grams
Total **Fat**	71	45	grams
Total **Saturated Fat**	20	15	grams
Total **Cholesterol**	279	263	milligrams
Total **Sodium**	2287	1198	milligrams
Total **Fiber**	12	8	grams
% **Calories from Fat**	28	27	

Apple Bread

A very tangy, tart-tasting bread with low calories, it has a strong apple flavor. This bread goes great with pork chops or pork roast.

INGREDIENTS

1½-Pound Recipe		1-Pound Recipe
2½ teaspoons	**active dry yeast**	1½ teaspoons
4 tablespoons	**sugar**	2½ tablespoons
2½ cups	**bread flour**	1¾ cups
¼ teaspoon	**nutmeg**	¼ teaspoon
1 teaspoon	**cinnamon**	½ teaspoon
½ teaspoon	**salt**	¼ teaspoon
½ cup	**whole-wheat flour**	¼ cup
1 tablespoon	**butter**	1 tablespoon
1 cup + 2 tablespoons	**apple sauce**	¾ cup

NOTE:
For Panasonic/National machines, use 3½ teaspoons of yeast for the 1½-pound loaf.

NUTRITIONAL ANALYSIS

	1½-Pound	1-Pound	
Total **Calories**	1864	1275	
Total **Protein**	53	35	grams
Total **Carbohydrates**	366	243	grams
Total **Fat**	20	17	grams
Total **Saturated Fat**	8	8	grams
Total **Cholesterol**	31	31	milligrams
Total **Sodium**	1077	540	milligrams
Total **Fiber**	14	8	grams
% **Calories from Fat**	10	12	

Whole-Wheat Oat-Cinnamon Raisin Bread

This bread combines the great taste and texture of whole wheat with the nutrition of oats and raisins for a naturally sweet loaf.

INGREDIENTS

1 1/2-Pound Recipe		1-Pound Recipe
2 teaspoons	**active dry yeast**	1 1/2 teaspoons
2 teaspoons	**gluten (optional)**	1 1/2 teaspoons
2 teaspoons	**dough enhancer (optional)**	1 1/2 teaspoons
2 cups	**whole-wheat flour**	1 1/2 cups
1 tablespoon	**cinnamon**	2 teaspoons
1/2 cup	**rolled oats**	1/4 cup
1 teaspoon	**salt**	1 teaspoon
2 tablespoons	**olive oil**	4 teaspoons
2 tablespoons	**honey**	4 teaspoons
1 cup	**warm water**	5 1/2 ounces
3/4 cup	**raisins**	1/2 cup

NOTES:

1. For Panasonic/National machines, use 3 1/2 teaspoons of yeast for the 1 1/2-pound loaf.
2. For best results, add the raisins at the end of the first mixing or use the mix cycle. If your machine has a mix cycle, add the raisins at the "mix" beep.

NUTRITIONAL ANALYSIS

	1 1/2-Pound	1-Pound	
Total **Calories**	1685	1166	
Total **Protein**	45	32	grams
Total **Carbohydrates**	327	228	grams
Total **Fat**	35	23	grams
Total **Saturated Fat**	5	3	grams
Total **Cholesterol**	0	0	milligrams
Total **Sodium**	2155	2147	milligrams
Total **Fiber**	43	30	grams
% **Calories from Fat**	19	18	

Cranberry Bread

The tart, tangy flavor of cranberries is predominant in this light, pink bread. A slice is excellent with meat, especially poultry or pork.

INGREDIENTS

$1^1/_2$-Pound Recipe		1-Pound Recipe
1 teaspoon	**active dry yeast**	$^1/_2$ teaspoon
$^1/_4$ cup	**sugar**	2 tablespoons
3 cups	**bread flour**	2 cups
2 teaspoons	**orange peel**	$1^1/_2$ teaspoons
$^1/_2$ teaspoon	**salt**	$^1/_2$ teaspoon
$^1/_2$ cup	**canned cranberries**	$^1/_4$ cup
3 ounces	**warm water**	$^1/_4$ cup
1 tablespoon	**olive oil**	2 teaspoons
3 ounces	**orange juice**	$^1/_4$ cup
1	**egg**	1
2 tablespoons	**chopped nuts**	4 teaspoons

NOTES:

1. For Panasonic/National machines, use 3 teaspoons of yeast for the $1^1/_2$-pound loaf.
2. Nuts are best added during the mix cycle, if your machine has one. If your machine does not have a mix cycle, you can either add the nuts at the beginning (with the rest of the ingredients) or after the initial mixing has taken place.

NUTRITIONAL ANALYSIS

	$1^1/_2$-Pound	1-Pound	
Total **Calories**	2098	1377	
Total **Protein**	59	41	grams
Total **Carbohydrates**	382	243	grams
Total **Fat**	35	25	grams
Total **Saturated Fat**	5	4	grams
Total **Cholesterol**	213	213	milligrams
Total **Sodium**	1158	1145	milligrams
Total **Fiber**	7	5	grams
% **Calories from Fat**	15	16	

Banana-Oat Bran Bread

This bread is nutricious and delicious, with a light banana flavor and a great oat texture.

INGREDIENTS

1 1/2-Pound Recipe		1-Pound Recipe
2 teaspoons	**active dry yeast**	1 1/2 teaspoons
2	**bananas**	1 1/2
2 cups	**bread flour**	1 1/2 cups
1/2 teaspoon	**salt**	1/4 teaspoon
5 tablespoons	**oat bran**	3 tablespoons
1/2 cup + 2 tablespoons	**oat flour**	1/4 cup + 2 tablespoons
1/2 teaspoon	**vanilla**	1/2 teaspoon
2 tablespoons	**olive oil**	4 teaspoons
2	**eggs**	2
1/2 cup	**warm water**	3 ounces
2 1/2 tablespoons	**honey**	2 tablespoons

NOTE:
For Panasonic/National machines, use 3 teaspoons of yeast for the 1 1/2-pound loaf.

NUTRITIONAL ANALYSIS

	1 1/2-Pound	1-Pound	
Total **Calories**	2103	1558	
Total **Protein**	64	49	grams
Total **Carbohydrates**	367	268	grams
Total **Fat**	46	34	grams
Total **Saturated Fat**	8	6	grams
Total **Cholesterol**	426	426	milligrams
Total **Sodium**	1203	667	milligrams
Total **Fiber**	23	15	grams
% **Calories from Fat**	20	20	

Apple Butter Bread

This is a sweet bread with a distinct apple flavor, enhanced with nuts.

INGREDIENTS

1½-Pound Recipe		1-Pound Recipe
2 teaspoons	**active dry yeast**	1½ teaspoons
½ cup	**sugar**	½ cup
1 teaspoon	**cinnamon**	½ teaspoon
3 cups	**bread flour**	2 cups
½ teaspoon	**salt**	¼ teaspoon
3 tablespoons	**warm water**	2 tablespoons
¾ cup	**apple butter**	½ cup
1	**egg**	1
1 teaspoon	**vanilla**	½ teaspoon
3 tablespoons	**butter**	2 tablespoons
½ cup	**chopped nuts**	¼ cup

NOTE:
For Panasonic/National machines, use 3½ teaspoons of yeast for the 1½-pound loaf.

NUTRITIONAL ANALYSIS

	1½-Pound	1-Pound	
Total **Calories**	2799	1767	
Total **Protein**	67	45	grams
Total **Carbohydrates**	445	280	grams
Total **Fat**	84	51	grams
Total **Saturated Fat**	27	18	grams
Total **Cholesterol**	306	275	milligrams
Total **Sodium**	1178	628	milligrams
Total **Fiber**	10	7	grams
% **Calories from Fat**	27	26	

Orange Bread

The light-orange color and aroma of this bread complement its distinctive orange flavor. It goes well with fruit salad, and it is great for breakfast toast.

INGREDIENTS

1½-Pound Recipe		1-Pound Recipe
1 teaspoon	**active dry yeast**	½ teaspoon
3 cups	**bread flour**	2 cups
½ teaspoon	**salt**	½ teaspoon
¼ cup + 1 tablespoon	**sugar**	3 tablespoons
1 tablespoon	**orange peel**	2 teaspoons
1	**egg**	1
2 tablespoons	**butter**	1½ tablespoons
3 ounces	**orange juice**	¼ cup
¾ cup	**warm water**	½ cup

NOTE:
For Panasonic/National machines, use 2½ teaspoons of yeast for the 1½-pound loaf.

NUTRITIONAL ANALYSIS

	1½-Pound	1-Pound	
Total **Calories**	2039	1385	
Total **Protein**	57	40	grams
Total **Carbohydrates**	369	242	grams
Total **Fat**	35	27	grams
Total **Saturated Fat**	17	13	grams
Total **Cholesterol**	275	260	milligrams
Total **Sodium**	1138	1135	milligrams
Total **Fiber**	6	4	grams
% **Calories from Fat**	15	18	

Carrot-Celery Bread

The light taste of celery and carrots combined with whole wheat makes this a great sandwich bread, especially for cold cuts. Try it with a bacon-lettuce-tomato sandwich for a unique treat.

INGREDIENTS

1½-Pound Recipe		1-Pound Recipe
1½ teaspoons	**active dry yeast**	1 teaspoon
1½ cups	**whole-wheat flour**	1 cup
1½ cups	**bread flour**	1 cup
½ cup	**grated carrots**	¼ cup
1 teaspoon	**salt**	½ teaspoon
1 teaspoon	**celery seed**	½ teaspoon
1 tablespoon	**olive oil**	2 teaspoons
2 tablespoons	**honey**	1½ tablespoons
1 cup	**warm water**	5½ ounces

NOTE:
For Panasonic/National machines, use 3 teaspoons of yeast for the 1½-pound loaf.

NUTRITIONAL ANALYSIS

	1½-Pound	1-Pound	
Total **Calories**	1635	1094	
Total **Protein**	52	34	grams
Total **Carbohydrates**	320	215	grams
Total **Fat**	21	14	grams
Total **Saturated Fat**	3	2	grams
Total **Cholesterol**	0	0	milligrams
Total **Sodium**	2160	1081	milligrams
Total **Fiber**	28	19	grams
% **Calories from Fat**	12	11	

Cheddar-Olive Bread

Olives and cheese have always been a great combination, and they are both present in this tasty bread. This was one of the tasters' favorites.

INGREDIENTS

1½-Pound Recipe		1-Pound Recipe
1½ teaspoons	**active dry yeast**	1 teaspoon
3 cups	**bread flour**	2 cups
4 teaspoons	**cornmeal**	1 tablespoon
1 teaspoon	**salt**	½ teaspoon
1 teaspoon	**basil**	½ teaspoon
1 tablespoon	**olive oil**	2 teaspoons
2	**eggs**	1
¾ cup	**warm water**	½ cup
½ cup	**sliced or grated black olives**	¼ cup
¾ cup	**grated cheddar cheese**	½ cup

NOTES:

1. For Panasonic/National machines, use 3 teaspoons of yeast for the 1½-pound loaf.
2. For DAK/Welbilt machines, use one extra tablespoon of warm water if the machine seems to labor with the 1½-pound loaf.
3. The dough will seem very stiff at first; however, once the cheese melts, the consistency will be about right.
4. For best results, add the olives during the mix cycle. If your machine does not have a mix cycle, add the olives after the initial mixing has completed.

NUTRITIONAL ANALYSIS

	1½-Pound	1-Pound	
Total **Calories**	2213	1441	
Total **Protein**	86	55	grams
Total **Carbohydrates**	314	209	grams
Total **Fat**	66	411	grams
Total **Saturated Fat**	25	16	grams
Total **Cholesterol**	515	273	milligrams
Total **Sodium**	3393	1786	milligrams
Total **Fiber**	10	6	grams
% **Calories from Fat**	27	26	

V-8 Bread

If you like tomato and V-8 juice, you'll like this bread. It uses V-8 juice as the liquid and combines that flavor with some seasonings to produce a light-orange bread with a distinctively vegetable taste.

INGREDIENTS

1 1/2-Pound Recipe		1-Pound Recipe
2 teaspoons	**active dry yeast**	1 1/2 teaspoons
1 1/2 teaspoons	**sugar**	1 tablespoon
3 cups	**bread flour**	2 cups
1 teaspoon	**dried onion**	1/2 teaspoon
1 teaspoon	**garlic powder**	1/2 teaspoon
3 tablespoons	**dry milk**	2 tablespoons
2 teaspoons	**Italian spice**	1 1/2 teaspoons
2 tablespoons	**Parmesan cheese**	1 1/2 tablespoons
1 teaspoon	**garlic salt**	1/2 teaspoon
3 tablespoons	**olive oil**	2 tablespoons
1/4 cup	**warm water**	1/4 cup
7 ounces	**V-8 juice**	5 ounces

NOTES:

1. For Panasonic/National machines, use 3 teaspoons of yeast for the 1 1/2-pound loaf.
2. If you like the taste but want to lower the salt content, buy salt-free V-8 juice and eliminate the garlic salt from the recipe.

NUTRITIONAL ANALYSIS

	1 1/2-Pound	1-Pound	
Total **Calories**	2085	1396	
Total **Protein**	63	42	grams
Total **Carbohydrates**	339	227	grams
Total **Fat**	51	34	grams
Total **Saturated Fat**	8	6	grams
Total **Cholesterol**	11	8	milligrams
Total **Sodium**	3084	1748	milligrams
Total **Fiber**	7	5	grams
% **Calories from Fat**	22	22	

Carrot Bread

This bread is bright orange in color. It has all the nutrients and flavor of fresh carrots. Prepare the carrot puree by steaming or boiling them. Then liquefy them in your blender or food processor.

INGREDIENTS

1½-Pound Recipe		1-Pound Recipe
1 teaspoon	**active dry yeast**	½ teaspoon
1 tablespoon	**sugar**	2 teaspoons
3 cups	**bread flour**	2 cups
½ teaspoon	**nutmeg**	¼ teaspoon
½ teaspoon	**salt**	¼ teaspoon
¾ cup	**carrot puree**	½ cup
1	**egg**	1
2 tablespoons + 1 teaspoon	**butter**	1½ tablespoons
3 tablespoons	**warm milk**	2 tablespoons
1½ tablespoons	**warm water**	1 tablespoon

NOTES:
1. For Panasonic/National machines, use 2 teaspoons of yeast for the 1½-pound loaf.
2. Be sure not to add the carrot puree while it is still hot from steaming. Let it cool so that you don't kill the yeast.

NUTRITIONAL ANALYSIS

	1½-Pound	1-Pound	
Total **Calories**	1907	1289	
Total **Protein**	59	41	grams
Total **Carbohydrates**	323	215	grams
Total **Fat**	40	27	grams
Total **Saturated Fat**	20	13	grams
Total **Cholesterol**	287	261	milligrams
Total **Sodium**	1190	1170	milligrams
Total **Fiber**	9	6	grams
% **Calories from Fat**	19	19	

Sweet Potato Bread

If you like yams on the dinner table, try this bread instead. It's a great supplement to a turkey dinner.

INGREDIENTS

1 1/2-Pound Recipe		1-Pound Recipe
1 1/2 teaspoons	**active dry yeast**	1 teaspoon
9 tablespoons	**brown sugar**	6 tablespoons
1/2 teaspoon	**ginger**	1/4 teaspoon
3 cups	**bread flour**	2 cups
1 teaspoon	**cinnamon**	1 teaspoon
1/2 teaspoon	**dried orange peel**	1/2 teaspoon
1 teaspoon	**salt**	1/2 teaspoon
1/4 cup + 2 tablespoons	**canned yams**	1/4 cup
3 ounces	**orange juice**	1/4 cup
3 ounces	**warm water**	1/4 cup
2	**eggs**	1
1 1/2 tablespoons	**butter**	1 tablespoon

NOTE:
For Panasonic/National machines, use 3 teaspoons of yeast for the 1 1/2-pound loaf.

NUTRITIONAL ANALYSIS

	1 1/2-Pound	1-Pound	
Total **Calories**	2359	1549	
Total **Protein**	65	41	grams
Total **Carbohydrates**	445	297	grams
Total **Fat**	35	22	grams
Total **Saturated Fat**	15	9	grams
Total **Cholesterol**	473	244	milligrams
Total **Sodium**	2320	1171	milligrams
Total **Fiber**	7	5	grams
% **Calories from Fat**	13	13	

Potato Bread

This is an old favorite, updated to use modern ingredients such as potato flakes. Still, the old fashioned flavor persists, and this bread is great with soups.

INGREDIENTS

1½-Pound Recipe		1-Pound Recipe
1 teaspoon	**active dry yeast**	½ teaspoon
2 tablespoons	**sugar**	4 teaspoons
2¾ cups	**bread flour**	2 cups
1 teaspoon	**salt**	½ teaspoon
4 tablespoons	**instant-mashed-potato flakes**	2½ tablespoons
¼ cup	**dry milk**	2 tablespoons
¼ cup	**buttermilk**	2½ ounces
2	**eggs**	1
2 tablespoons	**butter**	1 tablespoon
3 ounces	**orange juice**	¼ cup
5 ounces	**warm water**	3½ ounces

NOTES:

1. For Panasonic/National machines, use 2 teaspoons of yeast for the 1½-pound loaf.
2. For DAK/Welbilt machines, use ¾ cup of warm water for the 1½-pound loaf.

NUTRITIONAL ANALYSIS

	1½-Pound	1-Pound	
Total **Calories**	2073	1384	
Total **Protein**	79	51	grams
Total **Carbohydrates**	334	236	grams
Total **Fat**	44	24	grams
Total **Saturated Fat**	19	10	grams
Total **Cholesterol**	513	259	milligrams
Total **Sodium**	2727	1407	milligrams
Total **Fiber**	6	4	grams
% **Calories from Fat**	19	16	

Zucchini Bread

If one of your favorite summer vegetables is zucchini, here is a bread that will definitely have a place on your summer table.

INGREDIENTS

1 1/2-Pound Recipe		1-Pound Recipe
1 1/2 teaspoons	**active dry yeast**	1 teaspoon
1 1/2 tablespoons	**brown sugar**	1 tablespoon
1 3/4 cups + 3 tablespoons	**bread flour**	1 1/4 cups + 1 tablespoon
1/2 cup	**whole-wheat flour**	1/2 cup
1 cup	**shredded zucchini**	3/4 cup
1 teaspoon	**salt**	1/2 teaspoon
1 1/2 teaspoons	**ground coriander**	1 teaspoon
2 1/2 tablespoons	**dry milk**	1 1/2 tablespoons
1/4 cup	**wheat germ**	2 tablespoons
1 1/2 tablespoons	**butter**	1 tablespoon
5 1/2 ounces	**warm water**	3 1/2 ounces

NOTES:

1. For Panasonic/National machines, use 3 teaspoons of yeast for the 1 1/2-pound loaf.
2. For DAK/Welbilt machines, use 6 1/2 ounces of warm water in the 1 1/2-pound loaf.

NUTRITIONAL ANALYSIS

	1 1/2-Pound	1-Pound	
Total **Calories**	1580	1112	
Total **Protein**	58	40	grams
Total **Carbohydrates**	287	205	grams
Total **Fat**	27	18	grams
Total **Saturated Fat**	12	8	grams
Total **Cholesterol**	49	33	milligrams
Total **Sodium**	2231	1127	milligrams
Total **Fiber**	17	13	grams
% Calories from Fat	15	15	

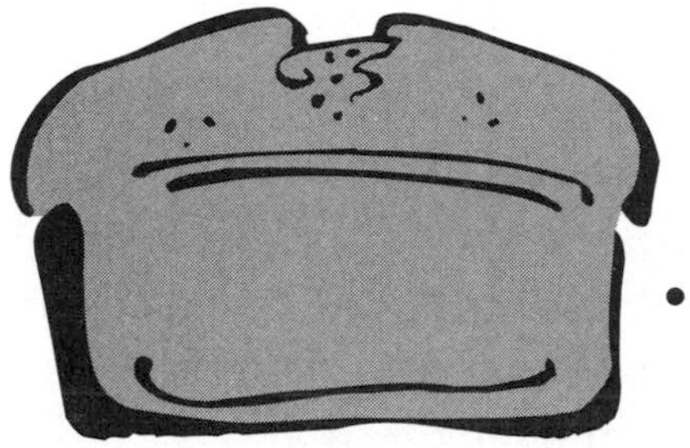

SOURDOUGH BREADS

Sourdough is a pioneer tradition in this country, made famous during the gold-rush days in California. Miners had to make bread, but they couldn't maintain leavening of any kind. So they made sourdough, a live mixture of fermenting bacteria that acted much like yeast. They kept their starter alive year after year (it really does get better with age) and used it daily for baking breads, biscuits, and pancakes.

All the recipes in this section use sourdough starter (see recipe on following page). Even with a bread machine, sourdough-bread recipes require a little more patience than other bread recipes because the sourdough batter must be prepared.

Sourdough Starter

This recipe will give you enough starter to begin with. Each time you remove starter to make batter, don't forget to replenish the starter with the leftover batter.

1. Warm a quart jar or similar container by filling it with hot tap water and letting it sit for a few minutes.
2. In a pan or microwave oven, heat 1 cup skim milk or low-fat milk to 100 to110 degrees/F. Then, remove it from the heat and add 3 tablespoons of plain yogurt to the mix.
3. Drain the warm water from the jar and wipe it dry.
4. Pour the milk-yogurt mixture into the jar and cover. It is better to use a plastic lid, but if your jar has a metal lid, place plastic wrap or waxed paper under the lid before screwing it tight.
5. Place the mixture in a warm place. Allow it to proof for 24 hours.
6. Stir 1 cup of all-purpose flour into the milk-yogurt mixture. Cover, and leave in a warm place to proof for 3 to 5 days.
7. At the end of 5 days, your starter should be bubbly and about the consistency of pancake batter. When it has reached this point, place the jar in the refrigerator for storage.

Here is the procedure for making the sourdough batter for your recipes:

1. Remove your sourdough starter from the refrigerator and allow it to reach room temperature (about 6 hours).
2. Place 1½ cups of starter in a 2-quart mixing bowl.
3. Return the remaining starter to the refrigerator.
4. Add 1½ cups of all-purpose flour and1 cup of warm skim milk and mix well. The batter should have the consistency of a light pancake batter.
5. Cover the bowl lightly and let the batter proof for 8 to12 hours in an 85 to 90 degree/F environment.
6. After proofing, use what batter you need for your bread (it can remain out for 1 to 3 days), but make sure you save at least 1½ cups of batter to replenish your starter.
7. Return the remaining batter to your starter pot. Stir and refrigerate.

Many people will place the starter directly into the ingredients. While this method will certainly work, it is not the best way to keep the starter active, because after you remove the starter, you have to add flour and milk and again proof the starter.

I have found it better to use the batter method described above. It tends to keep my starter more active and gives me plenty of batter to use in my recipes. If you use the batter method, place batter in the recipe any time sourdough starter is called for.

Sourdough French Bread

An old favorite, this bread has a long history. It's simple ingredients made it a favorite of the forty-niners and a San Francisco staple.

INGREDIENTS

1½-Pound Recipe		1-Pound Recipe
1½ teaspoons	**active dry yeast**	1 teaspoon
1 teaspoon	**sugar**	1 teaspoon
3 cups	**bread flour**	2 cups
1 teaspoon	**salt**	1 teaspoon
½ cup	**sourdough starter**	¼ cup
¾ cup	**warm water**	½ cup

NOTES:

1. For Panasonic/National machines, use 2½ teaspoons of yeast for the 1½-pound loaf.
2. If your machine has a "French bread" setting, use that setting for this recipe.

NUTRITIONAL ANALYSIS

	1½-Pound	1-Pound	
Total **Calories**	1758	1136	
Total **Protein**	59	38	grams
Total **Carbohydrates**	353	228	grams
Total **Fat**	8	5	grams
Total **Saturated Fat**	1	1	grams
Total **Cholesterol**	0	0	milligrams
Total **Sodium**	2141	2138	milligrams
Total **Fiber**	8	5	grams
% **Calories from Fat**	4	4	

Sourdough Rye Bread

This sourdough-and-rye combination is excellent for morning toast or for ham-and-cheese sandwiches. It has the flavor and texture of rye bread and a distinct sourdough aroma and taste.

INGREDIENTS

1 1/2-Pound Recipe		1-Pound Recipe
2 teaspoons	**active dry yeast**	1 1/2 teaspoons
2 1/2 cups	**bread flour**	1 1/2 cups
1 1/2 tablespoons	**unsweetened cocoa**	1 tablespoon
1 teaspoon	**salt**	1/2 teaspoon
2 teaspoons	**dill weed**	1 1/2 teaspoons
1 1/2 teaspoons	**caraway seed**	1 teaspoon
3/4 cup	**rye flour**	1/2 cup
1 tablespoon	**butter**	2 teaspoons
1	**egg**	1
2 teaspoons	**molasses**	1/2 tablespoon
1 tablespoon	**olive oil**	1/2 tablespoon
3 ounces	**warm water**	1/4 cup
1/2 cup	**sourdough starter**	1/4 cup

NOTE:
For Panasonic/National machines, use 3 teaspoons of yeast for the 1 1/2-pound loaf.

NUTRITIONAL ANALYSIS

	1 1/2-Pound	1-Pound	
Total **Calories**	2275	1473	
Total **Protein**	74	52	grams
Total **Carbohydrates**	401	256	grams
Total **Fat**	41	27	grams
Total **Saturated Fat**	12	8	grams
Total **Cholesterol**	244	234	milligrams
Total **Sodium**	2241	1148	milligrams
Total **Fiber**	9	6	grams
% **Calories from Fat**	16	16	

Sourdough Onion-Rye Bread

If you are looking for a tangy bread, look no further. This bread combines the tart flavor of sourdough with the distinct taste of onion, rye, and caraway seed. The result is a flavorful bread that is great for sandwiches. This was a favorite of the rye-bread tasters.

INGREDIENTS

1 1/2-Pound Recipe		1-Pound Recipe
1 1/2 teaspoons	**active dry yeast**	1 teaspoon
1 1/2 tablespoons	**gluten (optional)**	1 tablespoon
1 teaspoon	**caraway seeds**	1/2 teaspoon
1 1/2 cups	**bread flour**	3/4 cup
3 tablespoons	**onion-soup mix**	2 tablespoons
1 cup	**rye flour**	3/4 cup
1/2 cup	**whole-wheat flour**	1/4 cup
1/2 cup	**sourdough starter**	1/4 cup
2 tablespoons	**warm milk**	1 1/2 tablespoons
1 tablespoon	**olive oil**	2 teaspoons
1 tablespoon	**vinegar**	2 teaspoons
2 teaspoons	**molasses**	1 teaspoon
7 ounces	**warm water**	4 1/2 ounces

NOTE:
For Panasonic/National machines, use 3 teaspoons of yeast for the 1 1/2-pound loaf.

NUTRITIONAL ANALYSIS

	1 1/2-Pound	1-Pound	
Total **Calories**	1919	1137	
Total **Protein**	72	46	grams
Total **Carbohydrates**	364	212	grams
Total **Fat**	24	16	grams
Total **Saturated Fat**	3	2	grams
Total **Cholesterol**	1	1	milligrams
Total **Sodium**	2898	1918	milligrams
Total **Fiber**	15	8	grams
% **Calories from Fat**	11	13	

Sourdough Whole-Wheat Bread

Sourdough lovers will enjoy this variation of ordinary whole-wheat bread. This is a simple, low-calorie, low-fat bread that is nutritious as well as delicious.

INGREDIENTS

1½-Pound Recipe		1-Pound Recipe
1½ teaspoons	**active dry yeast**	1 teaspoon
1 tablespoon	**gluten (optional)**	2 teaspoons
1 tablespoon	**dough enhancer (optional)**	2 teaspoons
½ cup	**bread flour**	½ cup
2½ cups	**whole-wheat flour**	1½ cups
1 teaspoon	**salt**	1 teaspoon
1½ teaspoons	**olive oil**	1 teaspoon
1 cup	**warm water**	5½ ounces
½ cup	**sourdough starter**	¼ cup

NOTE:
For Panasonic/National machines, use 2½ teaspoons of yeast for the 1½-pound loaf.

NUTRITIONAL ANALYSIS

	1½-Pound	1-Pound	
Total **Calories**	1559	1152	
Total **Protein**	58	42	grams
Total **Carbohydrates**	318	231	grams
Total **Fat**	12	10	grams
Total **Saturated Fat**	2	2	grams
Total **Cholesterol**	0	0	milligrams
Total **Sodium**	2138	2137	milligrams
Total **Fiber**	40	25	grams
% **Calories from Fat**	7	8	

Sourdough Sesame Bread

This is a combination of sourdough and whole wheat, enhanced with the nutty flavor of sesame seeds. Serve it warm with any soup or salad.

INGREDIENTS

1½-Pound Recipe		**1-Pound Recipe**
1½ teaspoons	**active dry yeast**	1 teaspoon
½ cup	**sesame seeds**	5 tablespoons
1 cup	**whole-wheat flour**	¾ cup
1½ cups	**rye flour**	1 cup
1 teaspoon	**salt**	½ teaspoon
1	**egg**	1
2 tablespoons	**lemon juice**	4 teaspoons
2 tablespoons	**honey**	4 teaspoons
5 ounces	**warm water**	3½ ounces
½ cup	**sourdough starter**	¼ cup

NOTES:

1. For Panasonic/National machines, use 3 teaspoons of yeast for the 1½-pound loaf.
2. For DAK/Welbilt machines, use ¾ cup of warm water for the 1½-pound loaf.

NUTRITIONAL ANALYSIS

	1½-Pound	**1-Pound**	
Total **Calories**	2019	1346	
Total **Protein**	70	48	grams
Total **Carbohydrates**	337	223	grams
Total **Fat**	48	32	grams
Total **Saturated Fat**	7	5	grams
Total **Cholesterol**	213	213	milligrams
Total **Sodium**	2210	1139	milligrams
Total **Fiber**	23	16	grams
% **Calories from Fat**	21	21	

Sourdough Dill Bread

Here, you'll find the classic taste of dill bread with a trace of sourdough aroma. This is a splendid variation of dill bread that is excellent for sandwiches, particularly tuna salad.

$1\frac{1}{2}$-Pound Recipe	INGREDIENTS	1-Pound Recipe
$1\frac{1}{2}$ teaspoons	**active dry yeast**	1 teaspoon
2 tablespoons	**sugar**	$1\frac{1}{2}$ tablespoons
3 cups	**bread flour**	2 cups
1 teaspoon	**salt**	$\frac{1}{2}$ teaspoon
2 tablespoons	**dill weed**	4 teaspoons
1	**egg**	1
$\frac{3}{4}$ cup	**cottage cheese**	$\frac{1}{2}$ cup
3 ounces	**warm water**	$\frac{1}{2}$ cup
$\frac{1}{2}$ cup	**sourdough starter**	$\frac{1}{4}$ cup

NOTE:
For Panasonic/National machines, use $1\frac{1}{2}$ teaspoons of yeast for the $1\frac{1}{2}$-pound loaf.

NUTRITIONAL ANALYSIS

	$1\frac{1}{2}$-Pound	1-Pound	
Total **Calories**	2078	1377	
Total **Protein**	87	59	grams
Total **Carbohydrates**	383	249	grams
Total **Fat**	16	12	grams
Total **Saturated Fat**	4	3	grams
Total **Cholesterol**	236	228	milligrams
Total **Sodium**	2981	1653	milligrams
Total **Fiber**	8	5	grams
% Calories from Fat	7	8	

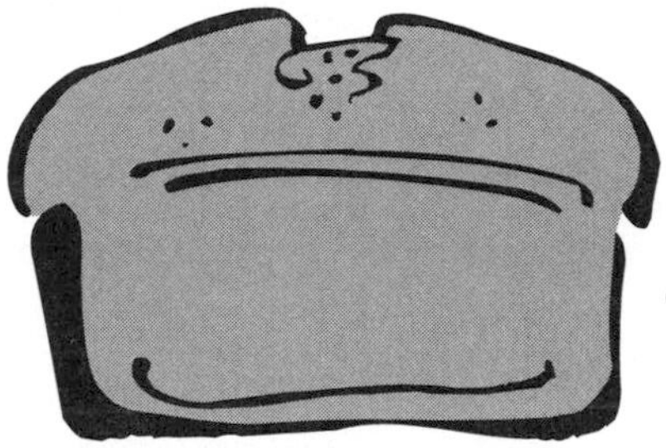

BREADS YOU FINISH YOURSELF

If you get tired of making the same-shaped breads and are willing to do a little bit of the work, you can use your machine to make the dough and then you can take it from there. Actually, any recipe in this book can be finished by hand, but this section primarily contains recipes that, because of their shape, can't be finished in the bread machine. Two of the recipes, French Bread and Bohemian Rye, could be finished in the machine, but are more authentic in their traditional shapes.

French Bread

A traditional French bread recipe, this is easy to make and yields a beautiful and tasty loaf.

INGREDIENTS

1½-Pound Recipe		1-Pound Recipe
2½ teaspoons	**active dry yeast**	1½ tablespoons
3 cups	**bread flour**	2 cups
1½ teaspoons	**salt**	1 teaspoon
1 cup	**warm water**	5½ ounces

NOTE:
For Panasonic/National machines, use 3 teaspoons of yeast for the 1½-pound loaf.

Instructions for baking: Remove from the machine after the first rise is complete (or use the dough cycle if your machine has one). After removal from the machine, knead the dough for 5 to 10 minutes. Shape the dough into a large loaf; then, place the dough on a baking pan or sheet that has been liberally sprinkled with cornmeal. Cover with a cloth and let the dough rise for 30 to 40 minutes.

After the bread has risen, use a sharp knife or razor blade to make diagonal cuts on the top of the loaf. Bake the loaf at 410 degrees for 30 to 40 minutes.

If a hard crust is desired, place a pan of water in the oven with the bread while it is baking. For a soft crust, cover the outside of the loaf with a water-and-egg mixture before baking.

To enhance the flavor and appearance, apply a fine spray of water before baking and then sprinkle the bread with a coating of sesame seeds.

NUTRITIONAL ANALYSIS

	1½-Pound	1-Pound	
Total **Calories**	1503	1001	
Total **Protein**	52	34	grams
Total **Carbohydrates**	300	200	grams
Total **Fat**	7	5	grams
Total **Saturated Fat**	1	1	grams
Total **Cholesterol**	0	0	milligrams
Total **Sodium**	3207	2138	milligrams
Total **Fiber**	7	5	grams
% **Calories from Fat**	4	4	

Pizza Dough

A high-rising pizza dough that makes one large pizza (using the 1½-pound recipe) or one medium pizza (using the 1-pound recipe). It is simple to make and lets you create your own pizza, using the toppings you like.

INGREDIENTS

1½-Pound Recipe		1-Pound Recipe
3 teaspoons	**active dry yeast**	2 tablespoons
3 tablespoons	**sugar**	1½ tablespoons
3 cups	**all-purpose flour**	2 cups
1 teaspoon	**salt**	1 teaspoon
3 teaspoons	**olive oil**	1½ teaspoons
1 cup	**warm water**	5½ ounces

NOTE:
Use the dough cycle, if your machine has one, or remove the dough from the bread machine after the first rise has been completed.

Instructions for baking: After removing the pizza dough from the bread machine, punch the dough down. Then place it in a greased bowl, cover it with a cloth, and let it rise in a warm place for 30 to 40 minutes.

Remove the dough from the bowl and roll it out flat. Place the dough on a pizza pan that has been sprinkled with cornmeal, and finish stratching the dough until it is a uniform thickness throughout. Spread tomato sauce on the pizza and finish with toppings of your choice. Bake the pizza at 350 degrees for 10 to 15 minutes or until the crust turns light brown.

NUTRITIONAL ANALYSIS

(Not including Pizza Toppings)

	1½-Pound	1-Pound	
Total **Calories**	1585	1064	
Total **Protein**	52	35	grams
Total **Carbohydrates**	301	201	grams
Total **Fat**	16	12	grams
Total **Saturated Fat**	2	2	grams
Total **Cholesterol**	0	0	milligrams
Total **Sodium**	2142	2139	milligrams
Total **Fiber**	7	5	grams
% **Calories from Fat**	9	10	

Breadsticks

Instead of sliced bread, try serving breadsticks with your spaghetti or lasagna dinner. These are easy and fun to make.

INGREDIENTS

$1\frac{1}{2}$-Pound Recipe		1-Pound Recipe
$1\frac{1}{2}$ teaspoons	**active dry yeast**	1 tablespoon
3 cups	**bread flour**	2 cups
$1\frac{1}{2}$ teaspoons	**salt**	1 teaspoon
1 cup	**warm water**	5 ounces
2 tablespoons	**olive oil**	4 teaspoons

NOTES:

1. For Panasonic/National machines, use 3 teaspoons of yeast for the $1\frac{1}{2}$-pound loaf. For DAK/Welbilt machines, use an extra 2 tablespoons of water with the $1\frac{1}{2}$-pound loaf.
3. Use the dough cycle, if your machine has one, or remove the dough from the bread machine after the first rise is completed.
4. Try substituting garlic salt for regular salt for a garlic-bread taste.
5. Add 3 tablespoons of onion soup mix for onion-flavored breadsticks.

Instructions for baking: Remove the dough from the machine and knead it for approximately 5 to 6 minutes, punching the dough to remove all the air. Form the dough into sticks by pinching balls of dough and rolling them with your hands into cylinder-shaped pieces. Lay the sticks in a pan (about 1 inch from each other) that has been dusted with cornmeal.

Let the breadsticks rise for approximately 45 minutes or until almost doubled in size. Bake them in a 375-degree oven for 15 to 20 minutes or until golden brown. For a crunchy crust, place a pan of water in the oven with the breadsticks while baking. If desired, brush a water-and-eggwhite mixture on the breadsticks before baking and coat with sesame seeds.

NUTRITIONAL ANALYSIS	$1\frac{1}{2}$-Pound	1-Pound	
Total **Calories**	1734	1156	
Total **Protein**	51	34	grams
Total **Carbohydrates**	300	200	grams
Total **Fat**	34	23	grams
Total **Saturated Fat**	5	3	grams
Total **Cholesterol**	0	0	milligrams
Total **Sodium**	3206	2137	milligrams
Total **Fiber**	7	4	grams
% **Calories from Fat**	18	18	

Bagels

These are traditional water bagels with a dense texture and great flavor. They are great in the morning with cream cheese or butter.

INGREDIENTS

$1^1/_2$-Pound Recipe		**1-Pound Recipe**
$2^1/_2$ teaspoons	**active dry yeast**	$1^1/_2$ teaspoons
3 cups	**all-purpose flour**	2 cups
$1^1/_2$ teaspoons	**salt**	1 teaspoon
$1^1/_2$ tablespoons	**sugar**	1 tablespoon
9 ounces	**warm water**	$^3/_4$ cup

NOTES:

1. For Panasonic/National machines, use 3 teaspoons of yeast for the $1^1/_2$-pound loaf. For DAK/Welbilt machines, use 10 ounces of warm water for the$1^1/_2$-pound loaf.
3. If your machine has one, use the dough cycle. If it does not, remove the dough at the end of the first rise.
4. For onion bagels, add 3 tablespoons of onion-soup mix.
5. For garlic bagels, use garlic salt instead of regular salt.

Instructions for baking: Remove the dough from the machine. Punch it down and knead it for 5 to 6 minutes. Then form into small (2 inches in diameter) balls. Flatten the balls slightly and use your thumb or finger to punch a hole into the middle of each bagel. Place the bagels on a lightly floured baking sheet, cover them with a cloth, and let rise for approximately 30 minutes.

In a pan, prepare a water-and-sugar mixture consisting of 6 cups of water and $^1/_2$ tablespoon of sugar. Bring the mixture to, and maintain, a steady boil. Boil each bagel for approximately 5 minutes in the solution, turning frequently. Then place the bagels on a baking sheet coated with cornmeal. Brush them with egg (whole eggs whipped) and bake in a 400-degree oven for 20 to 25 minutes or until brown.

NUTRITIONAL ANALYSIS	**$1^1/_2$-Pound**	**1-Pound**	
Total **Calories**	1572	1047	
Total **Protein**	52	34	grams
Total **Carbohydrates**	318	212	grams
Total **Fat**	7	5	grams
Total **Saturated Fat**	1	1	grams
Total **Cholesterol**	0	0	milligrams
Total **Sodium**	3207	2138	milligrams
Total **Fiber**	7	5	grams
% **Calories from Fat**	4	4	

Bohemian Rye Bread

This bread is made with 100-percent rye flour. Since rye flour doesn't rise much, it is best to bake this loaf in the traditional round shape. Rye lovers will enjoy its pure rye flavor and authentic Bohemian taste.

INGREDIENTS

1½-Pound Recipe		1-Pound Recipe
2 teaspoons	**active dry yeast**	1½ teaspoons
3 tablespoons	**gluten**	2 tablespoons
2 teaspoons	**sugar**	1½ teaspoons
2 teaspoons	**caraway seeds**	1½ teaspoons
3 cups	**rye flour**	2 cups
2 teaspoons	**salt**	1½ teaspoons
5 ounces	**warm water**	½ cup
½ cup	**sour cream**	¼ cup

NOTES:

1. For Panasonic/National machines, use 3 teaspoons of yeast for the 1½-pound loaf. For DAK/Welbilt machines, use 6 ounces of warm water for the 1½-pound loaf.
3. Use the dough cycle, if your machine has one, or remove the dough from the machine after the first rise is complete.

Instructions for baking: Remove the dough from the machine. Punch it down and knead it for approximately 5 to 6 minutes and then place it in a greased bowl. Cover the dough with a cloth and let it rise in a warm location for approximately 60 minutes. Remove from the bowl and shape it into a round or oblong loaf. Place the loaf on a baking sheet that has been liberally sprinkled with cornmeal. Cut two or three slits in the top of the loaf with a sharp knife or razor blade. Bake in a 375-degree oven for 30 to 35 minutes

NUTRITIONAL ANALYSIS	1½-Pound	1-Pound	
Total **Calories**	1700	1097	
Total **Protein**	83	55	grams
Total **Carbohydrates**	294	196	grams
Total **Fat**	37	20	grams
Total **Saturated Fat**	16	8	grams
Total **Cholesterol**	51	26	milligrams
Total **Sodium**	4336	3236	milligrams
Total **Fiber**	9	6	grams
% **Calories from Fat**	19	17	

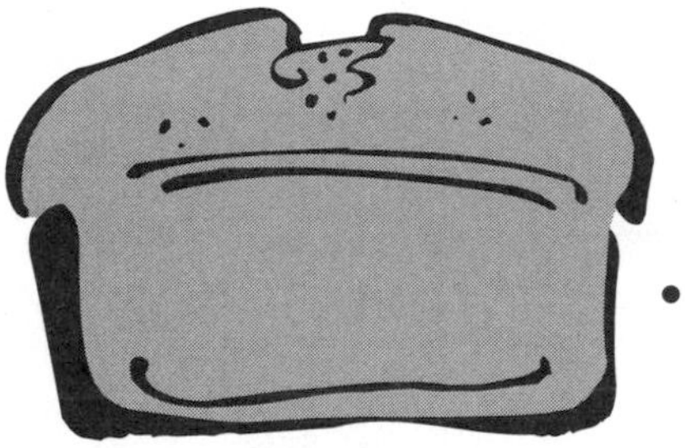

AMERICAN PIONEER BREADS

The recipes in this section are based on old American favorites from various parts of the United States. Because these recipes predate the commercial development of yeast for baking, most of these breads probably started out as baking-powder breads, baking-soda breads, or sourdough breads. In fact, the recipe for *Forty-Niner Sourdough Bread* has changed little since the days of the California gold rush.

Adobe Bread

Originally designed for the adobe ovens of the American Southwest, this bread tastes just as good when baked in your machine.

INGREDIENTS

1 1/2-Pound Recipe		1-Pound Recipe
1 1/2 teaspoons	**active dry yeast**	1 teaspoon
3 cups	**all-purpose flour**	2 cups
1 teaspoon	**salt**	1/2 teaspoon
3 tablespoons	**olive oil**	2 tablespoons
1 cup	**warm water**	5 ounces

NOTES:

1. For Panasonic/National machines, use 3 teaspoons of yeast for the 1 1/2-pound loaf.
2. For DAK/Welbilt machines, add 2 extra tablespoons of warm water to the 1 1/2-pound loaf.

NUTRITIONAL ANALYSIS

	1 1/2-Pound	1-Pound	
Total **Calories**	1853	1235	
Total **Protein**	51	34	grams
Total **Carbohydrates**	300	200	grams
Total **Fat**	48	32	grams
Total **Saturated Fat**	6	4	grams
Total **Cholesterol**	0	0	milligrams
Total **Sodium**	2140	1071	milligrams
Total **Fiber**	7	4	grams
% **Calories from Fat**	23	23	

Adobe Bread II

This is a variation of the adobe-bread recipe. The main difference is the addition of sugar and the deletion of olive oil.

INGREDIENTS

1 1/2-Pound Recipe		1-Pound Recipe
1 1/2 teaspoons	**active dry yeast**	1 teaspoon
3 cups	**all-purpose flour**	2 cups
2 teaspoons	**salt**	1 teaspoon
2 teaspoons	**sugar**	1 1/2 teaspoons
9 ounces	**warm water**	6 ounces

NOTES:

1. For Panasonic/National machines, use 3 teaspoons of yeast for the 1 1/2-pound loaf.
2. For DAK/Welbilt machines, use 2 extra tablespoons of warm water for the 1 1/2-pound loaf.

NUTRITIONAL ANALYSIS

	1 1/2-Pound	1-Pound	
Total **Calories**	1526	1020	
Total **Protein**	51	34	grams
Total **Carbohydrates**	307	206	grams
Total **Fat**	7	5	grams
Total **Saturated Fat**	1	1	grams
Total **Cholesterol**	0	0	milligrams
Total **Sodium**	4272	2137	milligrams
Total **Fiber**	7	4	grams
% **Calories from Fat**	4	4	

Amish Bread

Here is a simple, tasty, white bread with a sweet taste and a wonderfully fluffy texture.

INGREDIENTS

1½-Pound Recipe		1-Pound Recipe
1½ teaspoons	**active dry yeast**	1 teaspoon
3½ cups	**bread flour**	2 cups + 2 tablespoons
1 teaspoon	**salt**	½ teaspoon
3 tablespoons	**sugar**	2 tablespoons
4 tablespoons	**olive oil**	2½ tablespoons
9 ounces	**warm water**	6 ounces

NOTE:
For Panasonic/National machines, use 3 teaspoons of yeast for the 1½-pound loaf.

NUTRITIONAL ANALYSIS

	1½-Pound	1-Pound	
Total **Calories**	2233	1471	
Total **Protein**	55	37	grams
Total **Carbohydrates**	360	240	grams
Total **Fat**	62	39	grams
Total **Saturated Fat**	8	5	grams
Total **Cholesterol**	0	0	milligrams
Total **Sodium**	2140	1072	milligrams
Total **Fiber**	7	5	grams
% **Calories from Fat**	25	24	

Anadama Bread

The addition of cornmeal gives this rich white bread a somewhat crunchy texture.

INGREDIENTS

1 1/2-Pound Recipe		1-Pound Recipe
1 1/2 teaspoons	**active dry yeast**	1 teaspoon
1/2 cup	**cornmeal**	1/3 cup
1 teaspoon	**salt**	1/2 teaspoon
2 3/4 cups	**bread flour**	1 3/4 cups + 2 tablespoons
3 tablespoons	**molasses**	2 tablespoons
1 cup	**warm water**	6 ounces
2 1/2 tablespoons	**butter**	2 tablespoons

NOTES:

1. For Panasonic/National machines, use 3 teaspoons of yeast for the 1 1/2-pound loaf.
2. For DAK/Welbilt machines, add 2 tablespoons of warm water for the 1 1/2-pound loaf.

NUTRITIONAL ANALYSIS

	1 1/2-Pound	1-Pound	
Total **Calories**	2023	1403	
Total **Protein**	52	35	grams
Total **Carbohydrates**	364	247	grams
Total **Fat**	37	29	grams
Total **Saturated Fat**	19	15	grams
Total **Cholesterol**	78	62	milligrams
Total **Sodium**	2208	1117	milligrams
Total **Fiber**	13	9	grams
% **Calories from Fat**	17	18	

Cottage Cheese Bread

Pioneers used what they had on hand to make bread. This recipe uses ingredients found in the typical pioneer kitchen. Because the loaf will really rise, try the 1-pound recipe first to make sure your machine can handle the size.

INGREDIENTS

1½-Pound Recipe		1-Pound Recipe
1½ teaspoons	**active dry yeast**	1 teaspoon
¼ cup	**whole-wheat flour**	¼ cup
2¾ cups	**bread flour**	1¾ cups
1½ teaspoons	**salt**	1 teaspoon
½ teaspoon	**sugar**	½ teaspoon
1 tablespoon	**sour cream**	½ tablespoon
½ cup	**cottage cheese**	6 tablespoons
1	**egg**	1
2 tablespoons	**butter**	1 tablespoon
2 tablespoons	**honey**	1½ tablespoons
2 ounces	**warm milk**	1½ ounces

NOTE:
For Panasonic/National machines, use 3 teaspoons of yeast for the 1½-pound loaf.

NUTRITIONAL ANALYSIS

	1½-Pound	1-Pound	
Total **Calories**	1996	1357	
Total **Protein**	73	52	grams
Total **Carbohydrates**	330	229	grams
Total **Fat**	40	25	grams
Total **Saturated Fat**	20	11	grams
Total **Cholesterol**	298	260	milligrams
Total **Sodium**	3811	2610	milligrams
Total **Fiber**	10	8	grams
% **Calories from Fat**	18	16	

Country Bread

The specifics of the Midwestern origins of this bread are unknown, but it is a wonderfully rich white loaf sweetened by dates and nuts.

INGREDIENTS

1½-Pound Recipe		1-Pound Recipe
1½ teaspoons	**active dry yeast**	1 teaspoon
2 teaspoons	**dried lemon peel**	1½ teaspoons
3 tablespoons	**sugar**	1½ tablespoons
3 cups	**bread flour**	2 cups
1½ teaspoons	**salt**	1 teaspoon
2	**eggs**	1
5 tablespoons	**butter**	3 tablespoons
7 ounces	**warm milk**	5 ounces
3 tablespoons	**chopped nuts**	2 tablespoons
3 tablespoons	**chopped dates**	2 tablespoons

NOTES:

1. For Panasonic/National machines, use 3 teaspoons of yeast for the 1½-pound loaf.
2. Dates and nuts may be added during the mix cycle or add them at the beep (if your machine is equipped with one).

NUTRITIONAL ANALYSIS

	1½-Pound	1-Pound	
Total **Calories**	2609	1662	
Total **Protein**	75	48	grams
Total **Carbohydrates**	375	245	grams
Total **Fat**	90	55	grams
Total **Saturated Fat**	42	25	grams
Total **Cholesterol**	590	312	milligrams
Total **Sodium**	3448	2282	milligrams
Total **Fiber**	9	6	grams
% **Calories from Fat**	31	30	

Grumbera Bread

This bread was originally made with real mashed potatoes. For the sake of simplicity, I developed a recipe using mashed-potato flakes. It retains the excellent flavor and light-yellowish color of the original.

INGREDIENTS

1½-Pound Recipe		1-Pound Recipe
1½ teaspoons	**active dry yeast**	1 teaspoon
½ cup	**mashed-potato flakes or buds**	¼ cup
3 cups + 2 tablespoons	**bread flour**	2 cups + 2 tablespoons
1½ teaspoons	**salt**	1 teaspoon
2 tablespoons	**sugar**	1½ tablespoons
5 ounces	**warm water**	3 ounces
2	**eggs**	1
4 ounces	**warm milk**	3 ounces
1 tablespoon	**butter**	½ tablespoon

NOTE:
For Panasonic/National machines, use 3 teaspoons of yeast for the 1½-pound loaf.

NUTRITIONAL ANALYSIS

	1½-Pound	1-Pound	
Total **Calories**	2080	1356	
Total **Protein**	72	47	grams
Total **Carbohydrates**	360	243	grams
Total **Fat**	36	20	grams
Total **Saturated Fat**	12	6	grams
Total **Cholesterol**	462	232	milligrams
Total **Sodium**	3755	2427	milligrams
Total **Fiber**	7	5	grams
% **Calories from Fat**	16	13	

Indian Bread

Cornmeal and cream give this bread a distinctive flavor and texture.

INGREDIENTS

1½-Pound Recipe		1-Pound Recipe
1½ teaspoons	**active dry yeast**	1 teaspoon
2¼ cups + 2 tablespoons	**all-purpose flour**	1½ cups + 2 tablespoons
¾ cup	**cornmeal**	½ cup
1½ teaspoons	**salt**	1 teaspoon
2	**eggs**	1
3 tablespoons	**butter**	2 tablespoons
4 ounces	**cream**	2½ ounces
3 ounces	**warm water**	2 ounces
2½ tablespoons	**honey**	2 tablespoons

NOTE:
For Panasonic/National machines, use 3 teaspoons of yeast for the 1½-pound loaf.

NUTRITIONAL ANALYSIS

	1½-Pound	1-Pound	
Total **Calories**	2316	1520	
Total **Protein**	64	39	grams
Total **Carbohydrates**	343	233	grams
Total **Fat**	76	49	grams
Total **Saturated Fat**	41	26	grams
Total **Cholesterol**	570	307	milligrams
Total **Sodium**	3417	2261	milligrams
Total **Fiber**	12	10	grams
% **Calories from Fat**	30	29	

Plymouth Bread

An old New England favorite, this bread combines basic ingredients to produce a firm, tasty loaf.

INGREDIENTS

1 1/2-Pound Recipe		1-Pound Recipe
1 1/2 teaspoons	**active dry yeast**	1 teaspoon
2 3/4 cups	**bread flour**	2 cups
1 1/2 teaspoons	**salt**	1 teaspoon
4 tablespoons	**cornmeal**	2 1/2 tablespoons
4 tablespoons	**molasses**	2 1/2 tablespoons
1 1/2 tablespoons	**butter**	1 tablespoon
7 ounces	**warm water**	5 ounces

NOTE:
For Panasonic/National machines, use 3 teaspoons of yeast for the 1 1/2-pound loaf.

NUTRITIONAL ANALYSIS

	1 1/2-Pound	1-Pound	
Total **Calories**	1872	1316	
Total **Protein**	49	35	grams
Total **Carbohydrates**	354	249	grams
Total **Fat**	25	17	grams
Total **Saturated Fat**	12	8	grams
Total **Cholesterol**	47	31	milligrams
Total **Sodium**	3278	2183	milligrams
Total **Fiber**	9	6	grams
% **Calories from Fat**	12	11	

Southern Bread

This fluffy white-bread recipe has been a favorite in the southern United States. It's excellent sandwich bread.

INGREDIENTS

1 1/2-Pound Recipe		1-Pound Recipe
1 1/2 teaspoons	**active dry yeast**	1 teaspoon
2 tablespoons	**wheat germ**	5 teaspoons
1 tablespoon	**sugar**	1/2 tablespoon
3 tablespoons	**dry milk**	2 tablespoons
3 cups	**bread flour**	2 cups
1 teaspoon	**salt**	1/2 teaspoon
1 tablespoon	**butter**	1/2 tablespoon
9 ounces	**warm water**	6 ounces

NOTES:

1. For Panasonic/National machines, use 3 teaspoons of yeast for the 1 1/2-pound loaf.
2. For DAK/Welbilt machines, use 2 additional tablespoons of warm water for the 1 1/2-pound loaf.

NUTRITIONAL ANALYSIS

	1 1/2-Pound	1-Pound	
Total **Calories**	1755	1154	
Total **Protein**	61	42	grams
Total **Carbohydrates**	329	218	grams
Total **Fat**	20	12	grams
Total **Saturated Fat**	8	4	grams
Total **Cholesterol**	34	18	milligrams
Total **Sodium**	2236	1135	milligrams
Total **Fiber**	8	6	grams
% Calories from Fat	10	9	

War Bread

Legend has it that this bread was first baked during the American Revolution. Oats and cornmeal were added to make the flour go further, creating a great loaf of healthful bread.

INGREDIENTS

1½-Pound Recipe		1-Pound Recipe
1½ teaspoons	**active dry yeast**	1 teaspoon
2½ cups	**all-purpose flour**	1¾ cups
1 teaspoon	**salt**	1 teaspoon
¼ cup	**whole-wheat flour**	2½ tablespoons
¼ cup	**cornmeal**	2½ tablespoons
¼ cup	**rolled oats**	2½ tablespoons
10 ounces	**warm water**	7 ounces
1½ tablespoons	**molasses**	1 tablespoon
½ tablespoon	**butter**	½ tablespoon

NOTES:

1. For Panasonic/National machines, use 3 teaspoons of yeast for the 1½-pound loaf.
2. For DAK/Welbilt machines, use 2 additional tablespoons of warm water for the 1½-pound loaf.

NUTRITIONAL ANALYSIS

	1½-Pound	1-Pound	
Total **Calories**	1678	1165	
Total **Protein**	52	36	grams
Total **Carbohydrates**	330	226	grams
Total **Fat**	15	12	grams
Total **Saturated Fat**	5	4	grams
Total **Cholesterol**	16	16	milligrams
Total **Sodium**	2174	2160	milligrams
Total **Fiber**	15	10	grams
% **Calories from Fat**	8	9	

SPECIALTY BREADS For 2-Pound MACHINES

BASIC BREADS

The breads in this section are old favorites and basic breads that are fitting for any occasion. If you are new to bread machines, try the breads in this section first.

Air Bread

This recipe is based on a James Beard muffin recipe. Modifications to the thick muffin batter yield this slightly sweet-tasting white bread, which is great toasted.

INGREDIENTS	2-Pound	$1^1/_2$-Pound	1-Pound
warm water	10 ounces	$7^1/_2$ ounces	5 ounces
butter	$^1/_3$ cup	$3^1/_2$ tablespoons	$2^1/_2$ tablespoons
eggs	2	1	1
bread flour	4 cups	3 cups	2 cups
nonfat dry milk	$^1/_2$ cup	$^3/_8$ cup	$^1/_4$ cup
sugar	3 tablespoons	$2^1/_2$ tablespoons	$1^1/_2$ tablespoons
active dry yeast	2 teaspoons	$1^1/_2$ teaspoons	1 teaspoon

NUTRITIONAL ANALYSIS

	2-Pound	$1^1/_2$-Pound	1-Pound	
Total **Calories**	3026	2200	1496	
Total **Protein**	102	74	51	grams
Total **Carbohydrates**	470	356	235	grams
Total **Fat**	79	52	79	grams
Total **Saturated Fat**	42	27	20	grams
Total **Cholesterol**	536	297	263	milligrams
Total **Sodium**	1069	717	515	milligrams
Total **Fiber**	15	12	8	grams
% **Calories from Fat**	24	21	23	

Basic White Bread

This basic white bread recipe should work in most bread machines and should give you good results. Use it as a gauge to tell how well your machine operates.

INGREDIENTS	2-Pound	1½-Pound	1-Pound
warm water	6 ounces	4½ ounces	3 ounces
milk	6 ounces	4½ ounces	3 ounces
butter	2 tablespoons	1½ tablespoons	1 tablespoon
salt	2 teaspoons	1½ teaspoons	1 teaspoon
bread flour	4 cups	3 cups	2 cups
sugar	¼ cup	3 tablespoons	2 tablespoons
active dry yeast	1 teaspoon	1 teaspoon	½ teaspoon

NUTRITIONAL ANALYSIS

	2-Pound	1½-Pound	1-Pound	
Total **Calories**	2489	1870	1244	
Total **Protein**	73	55	37	grams
Total **Carbohydrates**	457	343	228	grams
Total **Fat**	38	28	19	grams
Total **Saturated Fat**	19	14	10	grams
Total **Cholesterol**	84	63	42	milligrams
Total **Sodium**	4597	3448	2298	milligrams
Total **Fiber**	14	11	7	grams
% **Calories from Fat**	14	14	14	

Cornmeal Bread

This is a Southwestern-type bread that is excellent with a bowl of chili or a taco salad.

INGREDIENTS	2-Pound	1 1/2-Pound	1-Pound
milk	1 1/3 cups	1 cup	2/3 cup
cottage cheese	1 cup	3/4 cup	1/2 cup
dried onions	1 1/3 tablespoons	1 tablespoon	2 teaspoons
green chili (diced)	3 tablespoons	2 tablespoons	1 1/2 tablespoons
cornmeal	7/8 cup	2/3 cup	1/2 cup
olive oil	1 1/3 tablespoons	1 tablespoon	2 teaspoons
sugar	1 1/3 tablespoons	1 tablespoon	2 teaspoons
bread flour	3 1/2 cups	2 2/3 cups	1 3/4 cups
active dry yeast	2 teaspoons	1 1/2 teaspoons	1 teaspoon

NUTRITIONAL ANALYSIS

	2-Pound	1 1/2-Pound	1-Pound	
Total **Calories**	2858	2164	1443	
Total **Protein**	114	86	57	grams
Total **Carbohydrates**	493	374	249	grams
Total **Fat**	44	33	22	grams
Total **Saturated Fat**	14	10	7	grams
Total **Cholesterol**	63	47	32	milligrams
Total **Sodium**	1097	823	549	milligrams
Total **Fiber**	14	10	7	grams
% Calories from Fat	14	14	14	

Egg Bread

A staple white bread, simple to make and smooth in texture.

INGREDIENTS	2-Pound	1 1/2-Pound	1-Pound
milk	1 cup	3/4 cup	1/2 cup
butter	1/3 cup	4 tablespoons	2 1/2 tablespoons
eggs	2	1	1
salt	1 teaspoon	3/4 teaspoon	1/2 teaspoon
bread flour	4 cups	3 cups	2 cups
active dry yeast	2 teaspoons	1 1/2 teaspoons	1 teaspoon

NUTRITIONAL ANALYSIS

	2-Pound	1 1/2-Pound	1-Pound	
Total **Calories**	2814	2079	1390	
Total **Protein**	88	63	44	grams
Total **Carbohydrates**	413	310	207	grams
Total **Fat**	87	63	42	grams
Total **Saturated Fat**	47	34	22	grams
Total **Cholesterol**	558	328	274	milligrams
Total **Sodium**	1476	2216	2990	milligrams
Total **Fiber**	15	12	8	grams
% **Calories from Fat**	28	28	27	

Egg Bread II

A slightly sweeter version of the previous Egg Bread recipe.

INGREDIENTS	2-Pound	1 1/2-Pound	1-Pound
warm water	2 ounces	1 1/2 ounces	1 ounce
butter	3/8 cup	1/4 cup	3 tablespoons
milk	2/3 cup	1/2 cup	1/3 cup
eggs	2	1	1
sugar	2 tablespoons	1 1/2 tablespoons	1 tablespoon
salt	1 teaspoon	3/4 teaspoon	1/2 teaspoon
bread flour	4 cups	3 cups	2 cups
active dry yeast	3 teaspoons	1 1/2 teaspoons	1 teaspoon

NUTRITIONAL ANALYSIS

	2-Pound	1 1/2-Pound	1-Pound	
Total **Calories**	2927	2114	1464	
Total **Protein**	85	61	43	grams
Total **Carbohydrates**	434	325	217	grams
Total **Fat**	92	61	46	grams
Total **Saturated Fat**	50	33	25	grams
Total **Cholesterol**	567	320	284	milligrams
Total **Sodium**	3030	2188	1515	milligrams
Total **Fiber**	15	12	8	grams
% **Calories from Fat**	28	26	28	

English Loaf

Breads don't come much simpler than this. The story is that an English food editor, Elizabeth David, developed this recipe when she became frustrated with the quality of the bread she was finding accompanying her gourmet meals. She developed this recipe to be simple, almost fool-proof, and to have a wonderful aroma while baking and a slightly salty taste.

INGREDIENTS	2-Pound	1½-Pound	1-Pound
warm water	12 ounces	9 ounces	6 ounces
bread flour	4 cups	3 cups	2 cups
salt	2 teaspoons	1½ teaspoons	1 teaspoon
active dry yeast	1 tablespoon	2¼ teaspoons	1½ teaspoons

NUTRITIONAL ANALYSIS

	2-Pound	1½-Pound	1-Pound	
Total **Calories**	2014	1510	1007	
Total **Protein**	70	53	35	grams
Total **Carbohydrates**	402	302	201	grams
Total **Fat**	10	7	5	grams
Total **Saturated Fat**	1	1	1	grams
Total **Cholesterol**	0	0	0	milligrams
Total **Sodium**	4291	3218	2145	milligrams
Total **Fiber**	17	12	8	grams
% **Calories from Fat**	4	4	4	

Herb Bread

This bread makes excellent toast and has the hint of flavor from several different herbs, mixed together here in a wonderful combination.

INGREDIENTS	2-Pound	1½-Pound	1-Pound
milk	6 ounces	4½ ounces	3 ounces
butter	2 tablespoons	1½ tablespoons	1 tablespoon
warm water	6 ounces	4½ ounces	3 ounces
sugar	3 tablespoons	2 tablespoons	1½ tablespoons
salt	2 teaspoons	1½ teaspoons	1 teaspoon
whole-wheat flour	4 cups	3 cups	2 cups
medium onion (chopped)	1	¾	½
dried dill weed	1 teaspoon	¾ teaspoon	½ teaspoon
rosemary (crushed)	1 teaspoon	¾ teaspoon	½ teaspoon
basil	1 teaspoon	¾ teaspoon	½ teaspoon
active dry yeast	1 tablespoon	2¼ teaspoons	1½ teaspoons

NUTRITIONAL ANALYSIS

	2-Pound	1½-Pound	1-Pound	
Total **Calories**	2143	1595	1072	
Total **Protein**	78	58	39	grams
Total **Carbohydrates**	405	300	202	grams
Total **Fat**	38	29	19	grams
Total **Saturated Fat**	19	15	10	grams
Total **Cholesterol**	84	63	42	milligrams
Total **Sodium**	5009	3756	2504	milligrams
Total **Fiber**	64	48	32	grams
% **Calories from Fat**	15	15	15	

Honey Bread

A simple, somewhat sweet bread that is great eaten fresh and warm.

INGREDIENTS	2-Pound	1 1/2-Pound	1-Pound
milk	1 cup	3/4 cup	1/2 cup
honey	3/8 cup	1/4 cup	3 tablespoons
butter	3 tablespoons	2 1/4 tablespoons	1 1/2 tablespoons
salt	1 teaspoon	3/4 teaspoon	1/2 teaspoon
bread flour	4 cups	3 cups	2 cups
active dry yeast	1 tablespoon	2 1/4 teaspoons	1 1/2 teaspoons

NUTRITIONAL ANALYSIS

	2-Pound	1 1/2-Pound	1-Pound	
Total **Calories**	2851	2106	1426	
Total **Protein**	79	59	40	grams
Total **Carbohydrates**	518	380	259	grams
Total **Fat**	52	39	26	grams
Total **Saturated Fat**	28	21	14	grams
Total **Cholesterol**	125	94	63	milligrams
Total **Sodium**	2620	1965	1310	milligrams
Total **Fiber**	17	13	17	grams
% **Calories from Fat**	16	16	16	

Oatmeal-Bran Bread

There are four favorite grains in this smoothly textured bread, a flavorful treat that makes excellent sandwich bread.

INGREDIENTS	2-Pound	1½-Pound	1-Pound
warm water	1⅓ cups	1 cup	⅔ cup
butter	3 tablespoons	2½ tablespoons	1½ tablespoons
molasses	2 tablespoons	1½ tablespoons	1 tablespoon
brown sugar	3 tablespoons	2½ tablespoons	1½ tablespoons
salt	1 teaspoon	½ teaspoon	½ teaspoon
dry milk	¼ cup	3 tablespoons	2 tablespoons
rolled oats	⅜ cup	¼ cup	3 tablespoons
bran	2 tablespoons	1½ tablespoons	1 tablespoon
whole-wheat flour	1 cup	¾ cup	½ cup
bread flour	3 cups	2¼ cups	1½ cups
active dry yeast	1 tablespoon	2¼ teaspoons	1½ teaspoons

NUTRITIONAL ANALYSIS

	2-Pound	1½-Pound	1-Pound	
Total **Calories**	2362	1998	1316	
Total **Protein**	83	62	41	grams
Total **Carbohydrates**	479	359	239	grams
Total **Fat**	46	37	23	grams
Total **Saturated Fat**	23	19	12	grams
Total **Cholesterol**	95	79	48	milligrams
Total **Sodium**	2629	1468	1314	milligrams
Total **Fiber**	34	25	17	grams
% **Calories from Fat**	16	16	16	

Finnish Easter-Crown Bread

see page 221

Rieska Bread II

• • •

see page 222

Olive, Mint, & Onion Bread

• • •

see page 223

Suomalaisleipaa Bread

• • •

see page 224

Pusstabrot

• • •

see page 226

Bohemian Christmas Bread

see page 225

Babovka

see page 227

Cuban Bread

• • •

see page 228

English Oatmeal Bread

• • •

see page 229

Irish Barmbrack

see page 230

Yorkshire Spice Bread

• • •

see page 231

Texas Bran Bread

• • •

see page 251

Old-Fashioned Buttermilk Bread

This buttermilk bread is a basic white bread with a thicker texture resulting from the use of buttermilk as the liquid instead of water.

INGREDIENTS	2-Pound	1½-Pound	1-Pound
buttermilk	14 ounces	10 ounces	7 ounces
honey	¼ cup	3 tablespoons	2 tablespoons
butter	2 tablespoons	1½ tablespoons	1 tablespoon
wheat gluten	1½ tablespoons	1½ tablespoons	2 teaspoons
bread flour	4 cups	3 cups	2 cups
salt	2 teaspoons	1½ teaspoons	1 teaspoon
active dry yeast	1 tablespoon	2¼ teaspoons	1½ teaspoons

NUTRITIONAL ANALYSIS

	2-Pound	1½-Pound	1-Pound	
Total **Calories**	2722	2028	1356	
Total **Protein**	102	74	50	grams
Total **Carbohydrates**	492	368	246	grams
Total **Fat**	37	28	19	grams
Total **Saturated Fat**	18	13	9	grams
Total **Cholesterol**	75	56	38	milligrams
Total **Sodium**	4963	3705	2480	milligrams
Total **Fiber**	6	4	3	grams
% Calories from Fat	12	12	12	

Onion-Caraway Bread

The fresh onion in this bread gives it a great aroma while baking.

INGREDIENTS	2-Pound	1 1/2-Pound	1-Pound
cottage cheese	1 1/3 cups	1 cup	2/3 cup
butter	1 tablespoon	2 teaspoons	1/2 tablespoon
warm water	5/8 cup	1/2 cup	5 tablespoons
sugar	1 1/3 tablespoons	1 tablespoon	2 teaspoons
salt	1 1/2 teaspoons	1 1/2 teaspoons	3/4 teaspoon
bread flour	4 cups	3 cups	2 cups
baking soda	1 teaspoon	3/4 teaspoon	1/2 teaspoon
chopped onion	1/4 cup	3 tablespoons	2 tablespoons
caraway seed	1 1/3 tablespoons	1 tablespoon	2 teaspoons
active dry yeast	2 teaspoons	1 1/2 teaspoons	1 teaspoon

NUTRITIONAL ANALYSIS

	2-Pound	1 1/2-Pound	1-Pound	
Total **Calories**	2482	1853	1241	
Total **Protein**	112	84	56	grams
Total **Carbohydrates**	436	327	218	grams
Total **Fat**	28	20	14	grams
Total **Saturated Fat**	12	9	6	grams
Total **Cholesterol**	56	39	28	milligrams
Total **Sodium**	5818	5153	2909	milligrams
Total **Fiber**	20	15	10	grams
% **Calories from Fat**	10	10	10	

Onion & Cheese Bread

This zesty bread has a moist consistency with the tangy flavor of cheddar and onion. Excellent bread for toasting.

INGREDIENTS	2-Pound	1½-Pound	1-Pound
water	14 ounces	1¼ cups	7 ounces
powdered milk	2⅔ tablespoons	2 tablespoons	1⅓ tablespoons
sugar	1⅓ tablespoons	1 tablespoon	2 teaspoons
salt	1 teaspoon	1 teaspoon	½ teaspoon
bread flour	4½ cups	3¼ cups	2⅛ cups
dried onions	1⅓ tablespoons	1 tablespoon	2 teaspoons
sharp cheddar cheese (shredded)	⅜ cup	¼ cup	3 tablespoons
active dry yeast	1½ teaspoons	1 teaspoon	½ teaspoon

NUTRITIONAL ANALYSIS

	2-Pound	1½-Pound	1-Pound	
Total **Calories**	2596	1888	1257	
Total **Protein**	92	67	48	grams
Total **Carbohydrates**	478	347	231	grams
Total **Fat**	30	22	15	grams
Total **Saturated Fat**	14	11	8	grams
Total **Cholesterol**	65	49	33	milligrams
Total **Sodium**	2502	1345	1251	milligrams
Total **Fiber**	4	3	2	grams
% Calories from Fat	11	11	11	

Onion-Mustard Bread

This is a tangy bread that is particularly good for sandwiches.

INGREDIENTS	2-Pound	1½-Pound	1-Pound
milk	1⅓ cups	1 cup	⅔ cup
prepared mustard	1½ tablespoons	1 tablespoon	2 teaspoons
olive oil	1 tablespoon	2½ teaspoons	½ tablespoon
eggs	2	1	1
sugar	1 tablespoon	2¼ teaspoons	½ tablespoon
salt	1 teaspoon	¾ teaspoon	½ teaspoon
bread flour	4 cups	3 cups	2 cups
black pepper	½ teaspoon	½ teaspoon	¼ teaspoon
minced onion	2 tablespoons	1½ tablespoons	1 tablespoon
active dry yeast	2 teaspoons	1½ teaspoons	1 teaspoon

NUTRITIONAL ANALYSIS

	2-Pound	1½-Pound	1-Pound	
Total **Calories**	2518	1871	1259	
Total **Protein**	91	66	46	grams
Total **Carbohydrates**	432	325	216	grams
Total **Fat**	43	32	22	grams
Total **Saturated Fat**	13	9	6	grams
Total **Cholesterol**	406	214	203	milligrams
Total **Sodium**	2738	2027	1369	milligrams
Total **Fiber**	17	12	8	grams
% **Calories from Fat**	16	15	16	

Poppy Seed Dilly Bread

"Dilly bread" is bread made with dill weed. This variation features plenty of interesting flavors with the addition of poppy seeds and onions.

INGREDIENTS	2-Pound	1½-Pound	1-Pound
warm water	1⅓ cups	1 cup	⅔ cup
butter	3 tablespoons	2 tablespoons	1½ tablespoons
bread flour	4 cups	3 cups	2 cups
instant dry milk	3 tablespoons	2 tablespoons	1½ tablespoons
sugar	2 tablespoons	2 tablespoons	1 tablespoon
dried onions	3 tablespoons	2 tablespoons	1½ tablespoons
dill weed	2 teaspoons	1½ teaspoons	1 teaspoon
poppy seeds	2 teaspoons	1½ teaspoons	1 teaspoon
salt	1 teaspoon	1 teaspoon	½ teaspoon
active dry yeast	2 teaspoons	1½ teaspoons	1 teaspoon

NUTRITIONAL ANALYSIS

	2-Pound	1½-Pound	1-Pound	
Total **Calories**	2521	1883	1261	
Total **Protein**	76	57	38	grams
Total **Carbohydrates**	444	338	222	grams
Total **Fat**	46	32	23	grams
Total **Saturated Fat**	23	15	12	grams
Total **Cholesterol**	94	63	47	milligrams
Total **Sodium**	2579	2433	1290	milligrams
Total **Fiber**	7	5	3	grams
% **Calories from Fat**	17	15	17	

Prune Bread

This is white bread with a zip to it. The addition of orange peel and chopped prunes gives it a mild fruit flavor that tastes great toasted and buttered.

INGREDIENTS	2-Pound	1 1/2-Pound	1-Pound
warm water	10 ounces	7 1/2 ounces	5 ounces
honey	2 tablespoons	1 1/2 tablespoons	1 tablespoon
salt	1 teaspoon	3/4 teaspoon	1/2 teaspoon
bread flour	3 1/2 cups	2 5/8 cups	1 3/4 cups
orange peel	1 teaspoon	3/4 teaspoon	1/2 teaspoon
prunes (chopped)	1 cup	3/4 cup	1/2 cup
active dry yeast	1 tablespoon	2 1/4 teaspoons	1 1/2 teaspoons

NUTRITIONAL ANALYSIS

	2-Pound	1 1/2-Pound	1-Pound	
Total **Calories**	2245	1684	1122	
Total **Protein**	66	50	33	grams
Total **Carbohydrates**	479	360	240	grams
Total **Fat**	9	7	5	grams
Total **Saturated Fat**	1	1	1	grams
Total **Cholesterol**	0	0	0	milligrams
Total **Sodium**	2163	1623	1082	milligrams
Total **Fiber**	25	19	13	grams
% **Calories from Fat**	4	4	4	

Quick Onion Bread

This easy bread has a great texture and wonderful onion flavor enhanced by the applesauce and honey.

INGREDIENTS	2-Pound	1½-Pound	1-Pound
water	1 cup	¾ cup	½ cup
applesauce	2 tablespoons	1½ tablespoons	1 tablespoon
honey	2 tablespoons	1½ tablespoons	1 tablespoon
eggs	2	1	1
dried onions	⅜ cup	¼ cup	3 tablespoons
bread flour	4 cups	3 cups	2 cups
powdered milk	1¼ teaspoons	¾ teaspoon	¼ tablespoon
salt	2 teaspoons	1½ teaspoons	1 teaspoon
active dry yeast	1 tablespoon	2 teaspoons	1½ teaspoons

NUTRITIONAL ANALYSIS

	2-Pound	1½-Pound	1-Pound	
Total **Calories**	2410	1765	1205	
Total **Protein**	86	61	43	grams
Total **Carbohydrates**	463	347	232	grams
Total **Fat**	21	13	10	grams
Total **Saturated Fat**	5	3	3	grams
Total **Cholesterol**	428	214	214	milligrams
Total **Sodium**	4432	3291	2216	milligrams
Total **Fiber**	8	6	4	grams
% Calories from Fat	8	7	8	

Wheat-Corn Bread

The combination of wheat flour, white flour, and cornmeal make this bread a tasty variation of ordinary white bread, with a bit of crunchy texture.

INGREDIENTS	2-Pound	1½-Pound	1-Pound
warm water	⅜ cup	¼ cup	3 tablespoons
honey	1 tablespoon	2¼ teaspoons	½ tablespoon
eggs	2	1	1
milk	1 cup	¾ cup	½ cup
butter	2 tablespoons	2 tablespoons	1 tablespoon
salt	1 teaspoon	¾ teaspoon	½ teaspoon
white corn meal	⅔ cup	½ cup	⅓ cup
wheat germ	⅜ cup	¼ cup	3 tablespoons
whole-wheat flour	1 cup	¾ cup	½ cup
bread flour	2½ cups	1¾ cups	1¼ cups
active dry yeast	2 teaspoons	1½ teaspoons	1 teaspoon

NUTRITIONAL ANALYSIS

	2-Pound	1½-Pound	1-Pound	
Total **Calories**	2680	1961	1340	
Total **Protein**	96	67	48	grams
Total **Carbohydrates**	459	332	230	grams
Total **Fat**	53	43	26	grams
Total **Saturated Fat**	24	21	12	grams
Total **Cholesterol**	456	267	228	milligrams
Total **Sodium**	2617	1993	1309	milligrams
Total **Fiber**	37	27	18	grams
% **Calories from Fat**	18	19	18	

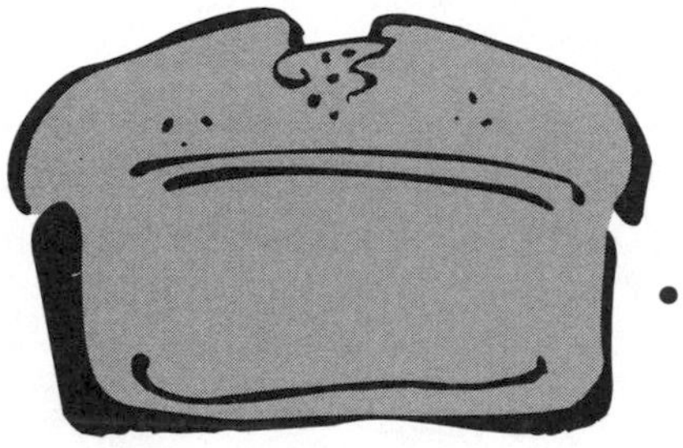

FESTIVE BREADS

These breads are traditional on special occasions or holidays.

Alpine Easter Bread

A tangy white bread with the nutty flavor of almonds and the zest of lemon.

INGREDIENTS	2-Pound	1½-Pound	1-Pound
milk	½ cup	⅜ cup	¼ cup
butter	½ cup	½ cup	4 tablespoons
warm water	2 ounces	1 ounce	1 ounce
eggs	2	1	1
vanilla extract	1 teaspoon	¾ teaspoon	½ teaspoon
lemon extract	½ teaspoon	¼ teaspoon	¼ teaspoon
sugar	½ teaspoon	½ teaspoon	¼ teaspoon
bread flour	4 cups	3 cups	2 cups
salt	1 teaspoon	½ teaspoon	½ teaspoon
dried lemon peel	2 teaspoons	1½ teaspoons	1 teaspoon
chopped almonds	2 tablespoons	1½ tablespoons	1 tablespoon
active dry yeast	2 teaspoons	1½ teaspoons	1 teaspoon

NUTRITIONAL ANALYSIS

	2-Pound	1½-Pound	1-Pound	
Total **Calories**	3128	256	1564	
Total **Protein**	88	64	44	grams
Total **Carbohydrates**	413	310	207	grams
Total **Fat**	122	112	61	grams
Total **Saturated Fat**	64	62	32	grams
Total **Cholesterol**	623	438	312	milligrams
Total **Sodium**	3243	2103	1621	milligrams
Total **Fiber**	17	12	8	grams
% **Calories from Fat**	36	40	36	

Cinnamon-Cranberry Bread

If you like the tart, distinctive taste of cranberries, you'll love this bread. It is only lightly sweetened, so the original flavor of the cranberries is highlighted.

INGREDIENTS	2-Pound	1 1/2-Pound	1-Pound
water	2 cups	1 1/3 cups	1 cup
vegetable oil	2 tablespoons	1 1/2 tablespoons	1 tablespoon
cinnamon	2 teaspoons	1 1/2 teaspoons	1 teaspoon
salt	1 tablespoon	2 teaspoons	1 1/2 teaspoons
dry milk	2 tablespoons	1 1/2 tablespoons	1 tablespoon
orange peel	2 tablespoons	1 1/2 tablespoons	1 tablespoon
sugar	2 tablespoons	1 1/2 tablespoons	1 tablespoon
bread flour	4 1/2 cups	3 1/4 cups	2 1/4 cups
active dry yeast	2 teaspoons	1 1/2 teaspoons	1 teaspoon
Add at mix cycle:			
fresh cranberries	1/2 cup	1/4 cup	2 1/2 tablespoons

NUTRITIONAL ANALYSIS

	2-Pound	1 1/2-Pound	1-Pound	
Total **Calories**	2690	1955	1345	
Total **Protein**	81	59	41	grams
Total **Carbohydrates**	488	351	244	grams
Total **Fat**	42	32	21	grams
Total **Saturated Fat**	7	5	4	grams
Total **Cholesterol**	15	12	8	milligrams
Total **Sodium**	6487	4332	3243	milligrams
Total **Fiber**	7	5	4	grams
% **Calories from Fat**	14	15	14	

Cinnamon Swirl Orange Bread

This glazed bread is excellent for an after-dinner treat.

INGREDIENTS	2-Pound	1 1/2-Pound	1-Pound
warm water	3 tablespoons	2 1/2 tablespoons	1 1/2 tablespoons
milk	1/2 cup	3/8 cup	1/4 cup
margarine	2 tablespoons	1 1/2 tablespoons	1 tablespoon
orange juice	1/2 cup	3/8 cup	1/4 cup
eggs	2	1	1
sugar	1/4 cup	3 tablespoons	2 tablespoons
salt	1 teaspoon	3/4 teaspoon	1/2 teaspoon
bread flour	4 cups	3 cups	2 cups
cinnamon	1 tablespoon	2 1/4 teaspoons	1/2 tablespoon
active dry yeast	1 tablespoon	2 1/4 teaspoons	1 1/2 teaspoons
orange peel (grated)	1 tablespoon	2 1/4 teaspoons	1/2 tablespoon

NUTRITIONAL ANALYSIS

	2-Pound	1 1/2-Pound	1-Pound	
Total **Calories**	2685	1982	1343	
Total **Protein**	86	62	43	grams
Total **Carbohydrates**	479	359	239	grams
Total **Fat**	45	32	23	grams
Total **Saturated Fat**	11	7	5	grams
Total **Cholesterol**	378	193	189	milligrams
Total **Sodium**	2587	1913	1293	milligrams
Total **Fiber**	21	16	10	grams
% Calories from Fat	15	15	15	

Honey-Mustard Bread

This is a great sandwich bread with a light wheat consistency and the distinctive flavors of honey and mustard.

INGREDIENTS	2-Pound	1 1/2-Pound	1-Pound
water	1 cup	3/4 cup	1/2 cup
honey	1/3 cup	3 1/2 tablespoons	2 1/2 tablespoons
chicken broth	1/2 cup	3/8 cup	1/4 cup
honey mustard	3 1/3 tablespoons	2 1/2 tablespoons	5 teaspoons
bread flour	3 cups	2 1/4 cups	1 1/2 cups
whole-wheat flour	1 cup	3/4 cup	1/2 cup
dry milk	1 1/3 tablespoons	1 tablespoon	2 teaspoons
chives (dried)	2 teaspoons	1 1/2 teaspoons	1 teaspoon
salt	1 teaspoon	3/4 teaspoon	1/2 teaspoon
active dry yeast	4 teaspoons	1 teaspoon	1/2 teaspoon

NUTRITIONAL ANALYSIS

	2-Pound	1 1/2-Pound	1-Pound	
Total **Calories**	2367	1758	1183	
Total **Protein**	84	63	42	grams
Total **Carbohydrates**	486	360	243	grams
Total **Fat**	15	11	8	grams
Total **Saturated Fat**	2	1	1	grams
Total **Cholesterol**	2	2	1	milligrams
Total **Sodium**	3660	2745	1830	milligrams
Total **Fiber**	21	16	10	grams
% **Calories from Fat**	6	6	6	

Multigrain Garlic-Dill Bread

This is a flavorful variation on a basic bread. The garlic, dill weed, and yogurt add a particular zest to the loaf.

INGREDIENTS	2-Pound	1 1/2-Pound	1-Pound
warm water	1 cup	3/4 cup	1/2 cup
plain yogurt	2/3 cup	1/2 cup	1/3 cup
olive oil	2 tablespoons	1 1/2 tablespoons	1 tablespoon
rolled oats	1/2 cup	3/8 cup	1/4 cup
cracked wheat	1/2 cup	3/8 cup	1/4 cup
brown sugar	1 tablespoon	2 1/4 teaspoons	1 1/2 teaspoons
salt	1 1/2 teaspoons	1 1/4 teaspoons	3/4 teaspoon
bread flour	3 1/2 cups	2 3/4 cups	1 3/4 cups
minced garlic	1 tablespoon	2 1/4 teaspoons	1 1/2 teaspoons
dill weed	2 teaspoons	1 1/2 teaspoons	1 teaspoon
active dry yeast	2 teaspoons	1 teaspoon	1 teaspoon

NUTRITIONAL ANALYSIS

	2-Pound	1 1/2-Pound	1-Pound	
Total **Calories**	2293	1781	1146	
Total **Protein**	73	57	37	grams
Total **Carbohydrates**	398	311	199	grams
Total **Fat**	43	33	22	grams
Total **Saturated Fat**	9	6	4	grams
Total **Cholesterol**	19	14	10	milligrams
Total **Sodium**	3299	2741	1650	milligrams
Total **Fiber**	18	14	9	grams
% **Calories from Fat**	17	17	17	

Peanut Butter Bread

The peanut butter in this bread gives it a smooth texture. It is excellent for toasting.

INGREDIENTS	2-Pound	1 1/2-Pound	1-Pound
eggs	2	1	1
milk	12 ounces	9 ounces	6 ounces
bread flour	4 cups	3 cups	2 cups
salt	1 teaspoon	3/4 teaspoon	1/2 teaspoon
sugar	1 cup	3/4 cup	1/2 cup
peanut butter	1 1/2 cups	1 1/8 cups	3/4 cup
active dry yeast	2 teaspoons	1 1/2 teaspoons	1 teaspoon

NUTRITIONAL ANALYSIS

	2-Pound	1 1/2-Pound	1-Pound	
Total **Calories**	5387	4009	2694	
Total **Protein**	186	137	93	grams
Total **Carbohydrates**	697	523	349	grams
Total **Fat**	223	165	111	grams
Total **Saturated Fat**	48	36	24	grams
Total **Cholesterol**	408	215	204	milligrams
Total **Sodium**	4272	3177	2136	milligrams
Total **Fiber**	38	29	19	grams
% **Calories from Fat**	36	36	36	

FESTIVE BREADS

Poppy Seed Loaf

A great party bread that is especially good on the table with other finger foods.

(Make poppy seed dip for the bread by combining 4 tablespoons of melted butter and 1/4 cup of poppy seeds. Get the bread from the bread machine while warm, tear or cut pieces from the loaf, and dip.)

INGREDIENTS	2-Pound	1 1/2-Pound	1-Pound
warm water	1 cup	3/4 cup	1/2 cup
milk	1/2 cup	3/8 cup	1/4 cup
shortening	1 tablespoon	2 teaspoons	1/2 tablespoon
salt	1 teaspoon	3/4 teaspoon	1/2 teaspoon
sugar	2 tablespoons	1 1/2 tablespoons	1 tablespoon
bread flour	4 cups	3 cups	2 cups
poppy seeds	1 tablespoon	2 1/4 teaspoons	1/2 tablespoon
active dry yeast	2 teaspoons	1 1/2 teaspoons	1 teaspoon

NUTRITIONAL ANALYSIS

	2-Pound	1 1/2-Pound	1-Pound	
Total **Calories**	2334	1741	1167	
Total **Protein**	74	56	37	grams
Total **Carbohydrates**	433	325	217	grams
Total **Fat**	30	22	15	grams
Total **Saturated Fat**	8	5	4	grams
Total **Cholesterol**	17	12	8	milligrams
Total **Sodium**	2216	1662	1108	milligrams
Total **Fiber**	18	14	9	grams
% **Calories from Fat**	12	11	12	

Soft Cheese Bread

This bread has the soft, spongy texture of oatmeal bread with the pizzazz of tangy cheese.

INGREDIENTS	2-Pound	1½-Pound	1-Pound
water	1 cup	¾ cup	½ cup
sharp cheddar cheese (shredded)	1⅓ cups	1 cup	⅔ cup
eggs	2	1	1
olive oil	1⅓ tablespoons	1 tablespoon	2 teaspoons
bread flour	3½ cups	2½ cups	1⅔ cups
rolled oats	1⅓ cups	1 cup	⅔ cup
powdered milk	⅓ cup	¼ cup	2⅔ tablespoons
salt	2 teaspoons	1½ teaspoons	1 teaspoon
sugar	1⅓ tablespoons	1 tablespoon	2 teaspoons
active dry yeast	2 teaspoons	1½ teaspoons	1 teaspoon

NUTRITIONAL ANALYSIS

	2-Pound	1½-Pound	1-Pound	
Total **Calories**	3362	2422	1640	
Total **Protein**	139	99	68	grams
Total **Carbohydrates**	459	332	221	grams
Total **Fat**	105	76	52	grams
Total **Saturated Fat**	47	34	24	grams
Total **Cholesterol**	625	363	313	milligrams
Total **Sodium**	5511	4103	2755	milligrams
Total **Fiber**	15	12	7	grams
% Calories from Fat	28	28	29	

Sweet Potato-Wheat Twist

A soft-textured bread with a distinctive sweet potato flavor. Excellent with soup.

INGREDIENTS	2-Pound	1½-Pound	1-Pound
warm water	⅓ cup	3¾ tablespoons	2½ tablespoons
yams	⅔ cup	½ cup	⅓ cup
buttermilk	½ cup	⅜ cup	¼ cup
butter	1 tablespoon	1 tablespoon	½ tablespoon
honey	1 tablespoon	2½ teaspoons	½ tablespoon
eggs	2	1	1
salt	1 teaspoon	¾ teaspoon	½ teaspoon
bread flour	3½ cups	2⅝ cups	1¾ cups
whole-wheat flour	1 cup	¾ cup	½ cup
active dry yeast	1 tablespoon	2¼ teaspoons	1½ teaspoons

NUTRITIONAL ANALYSIS

	2-Pound	1½-Pound	1-Pound	
Total **Calories**	2616	1961	1308	
Total **Protein**	95	68	47	grams
Total **Carbohydrates**	488	367	244	grams
Total **Fat**	32	25	16	grams
Total **Saturated Fat**	12	10	6	grams
Total **Cholesterol**	396	215	198	milligrams
Total **Sodium**	2516	1889	1258	milligrams
Total **Fiber**	33	25	17	grams
% Calories from Fat	11	11	11	

Three Kings Bread

Called *Rosca de los Reyes* in Latin America, this bread is customarily baked to celebrate Twelfth Night (January 6th). In its normal form, the bread is baked in a ring shape and garnished with nuts and candied fruits. Often a tiny doll or an uncooked lima bean is hidden in the bread. The person receiving the bean or doll hosts a party on February 2nd, *El dia de la candelaria.*

INGREDIENTS	2-Pound	1½-Pound	1-Pound
warm water	⅔ cup	½ cup	⅓ cup
butter	½ cup	½ cup	4 tablespoons
eggs	2	1	1
bread flour	3½ cups	2⅝ cups	1¾ cups
dry milk	3 tablespoons	2½ tablespoons	1½ tablespoons
sugar	¼ cup	3 tablespoons	2 tablespoons
salt	1 teaspoon	¾ teaspoon	½ teaspoon
raisins	⅓ cup	3½ tablespoons	2½ tablespoons
walnuts (chopped)	⅓ cup	4 tablespoons	2½ tablespoons
candied cherries (chopped)	2 tablespoons	1⅓ tablespoons	1 tablespoon
orange peel (grated)	2 teaspoons	1½ teaspoons	1 teaspoon
lemon rind (grated)	2 teaspoons	1½ teaspoons	1 teaspoon
active dry yeast	1 tablespoon	2¼ teaspoons	1½ teaspoons

NUTRITIONAL ANALYSIS

	2-Pound	1½-Pound	1-Pound	
Total **Calories**	3177	2542	1582	
Total **Protein**	82	60	41	grams
Total **Carbohydrates**	461	342	229	grams
Total **Fat**	114	106	57	grams
Total **Saturated Fat**	61	59	31	grams
Total **Cholesterol**	609	428	34	milligrams
Total **Sodium**	3277	2667	1638	milligrams
Total **Fiber**	18	13	9	grams
% **Calories from Fat**	32	37	32	

Wild Rice Bread

Wild rice is difficult to find growing wild, and hence fairly expensive. This recipe is made even better if you can use wild rice flour instead of the regular rice flour called for. If you have a grinder or food processor that can process grains into flour, you can simply make your own wild rice flour. Otherwise, use the commercially available rice flour and use the cooked wild rice to give the bread the wild rice flavor. Be sure to drain the cooked rice well and let it dry for a while before using it in the recipe. The cooked wild rice is included as a dry ingredient in the ratio, so you don't want wet rice or your bread will not rise properly.

INGREDIENTS	2-Pound	1 1/2-Pound	1-Pound
warm water	1 1/2 cups	9 ounces	3/4 cup
vegetable oil	3 tablespoons	2 1/2 tablespoons	1 1/2 tablespoons
rice flour	1/2 cup	3/8 cup	1/4 cup
salt	1 teaspoon	3/4 teaspoon	1/2 teaspoon
bread flour	3 cups	2 1/2 cups	1 1/2 cups
cooked wild rice	2/3 cup	1/2 cup	1/3 cup
active dry yeast	2 teaspoons	1 1/2 teaspoons	1 teaspoon

NUTRITIONAL ANALYSIS

	2-Pound	1 1/2-Pound	1-Pound	
Total **Calories**	2268	1855	1134	
Total **Protein**	61	50	31	grams
Total **Carbohydrates**	388	316	194	grams
Total **Fat**	50	41	25	grams
Total **Saturated Fat**	6	5	3	grams
Total **Cholesterol**	0	0	0	milligrams
Total **Sodium**	2158	1619	1079	milligrams
Total **Fiber**	16	13	8	grams
% **Calories from Fat**	20	20	20	

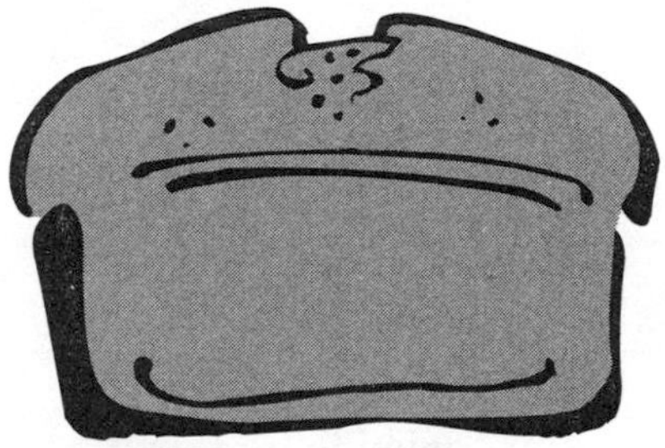

INTERNATIONAL BREADS

These breads have their origins all around the world. Many are traditional loaves of their respective countries, modified for baking in the bread machine.

Panettone

Because it has a sweet, nutty flavor, this Italian bread is particularly enjoyable as a breakfast toast served with butter and jam.

INGREDIENTS

1 1/2-Pound		1-Pound
1 1/2 teaspoons	**active dry yeast**	1 teaspoon
1/2 teaspoon	**dried orange peel**	1/2 teaspoon
1 1/2 teaspoons	**dried lemon peel**	1 teaspoon
1/2 teaspoon	**salt**	1/2 teaspoon
3 cups + 3 tablespoons	**all-purpose flour**	2 cups + 2 tablespoons
6 tablespoons	**sugar**	4 tablespoons
2	**eggs**	1
7 1/2 tablespoons	**butter**	5 tablespoons
6 ounces	**warm milk**	1/2 cup
6 tablespoons	**raisins**	4 tablespoons
4 tablespoons	**shredded almonds**	3 tablespoons

NOTES:

1. For Panasonic/National machines, use 3 teaspoons of yeast for the 1 1/2-pound loaf.
2. If your machine has a mix cycle, you may add the almonds and raisins at the beep.

NUTRITIONAL ANALYSIS

	1 1/2-Pound	1-Pound	
Total **Calories**	3196	2060	
Total **Protein**	79	49	grams
Total **Carbohydrates**	448	287	grams
Total **Fat**	124	82	grams
Total **Saturated Fat**	60	40	grams
Total **Cholesterol**	666	373	milligrams
Total **Sodium**	1310	1208	milligrams
Total **Fiber**	11	7	grams
% **Calories from Fat**	35	36	

Ethiopian Spice Bread

The distinct and unusual blend of spices in this bread make it a great choice with soups or salads.

INGREDIENTS

1 1/2-Pound		1-Pound
1 1/2 teaspoons	**active dry yeast**	1 teaspoon
3 cups	**all-purpose flour**	2 cups
1/2 teaspoon	**paprika**	1/2 teaspoon
1/2 teaspoon	**salt**	1/2 teaspoon
1/2 teaspoon	**ground cardamom**	1/2 teaspoon
1 tablespoon	**ground coriander**	2 teaspoons
1/2 teaspoon	**garlic salt**	1/2 teaspoon
1 1/2 teaspoons	**dried onion**	1 teaspoon
1 teaspoon	**hot sauce (red pepper)**	1/2 teaspoon
5 1/2 tablespoons	**butter**	1/2 tablespoon
7 ounces	**warm water**	4 1/2 ounces

NOTES:

1. For Panasonic/National machines, use 3 teaspoons of yeast for the 1 1/2-pound loaf.
2. For DAK/Welbilt machines, use 2 additional tablespoons of warm water for the 1 1/2-pound loaf.

NUTRITIONAL ANALYSIS

	1 1/2-Pound	1-Pound	
Total **Calories**	2072	1365	
Total **Protein**	52	35	grams
Total **Carbohydrates**	305	204	grams
Total **Fat**	71	45	grams
Total **Saturated Fat**	40	26	grams
Total **Cholesterol**	171	109	milligrams
Total **Sodium**	2239	2189	milligrams
Total **Fiber**	8	6	grams
% Calories from Fat	31	30	

Chive & Garlic Bread

This is a zippy variation of white bread that is fantastic with pasta or soups. Sauté the garlic in butter for 1 to 2 minutes; then let cool before adding to the mixture.

INGREDIENTS	2-Pound	1 1/2-Pound	1-Pound
butter	1 1/2 tablespoons	1 tablespoon	2 teaspoons
milk	14 ounces	1 1/4 cups	7 ounces
cloves garlic	6	5	3
bread flour	4 cups	3 cups	2 cups
parmesan cheese (grated)	1/2 cup	1/3 cup	3 1/3 tablespoons
fresh chives (chopped)	3 tablespoons	2 tablespoons	1 1/2 tablespoons
sugar	1 1/2 tablespoons	1 tablespoon	2 teaspoons
salt	1 teaspoon	3/4 teaspoon	1/2 teaspoon
active dry yeast	2 teaspoons	1 teaspoon	1/2 teaspoon

NUTRITIONAL ANALYSIS

	2-Pound	1 1/2-Pound	1-Pound	
Total **Calories**	2700	2007	1332	
Total **Protein**	102	76	50	grams
Total **Carbohydrates**	446	333	221	grams
Total **Fat**	53	39	26	grams
Total **Saturated Fat**	29	21	14	grams
Total **Cholesterol**	135	98	65	milligrams
Total **Sodium**	3344	2496	1661	milligrams
Total **Fiber**	5	3	2	grams
% Calories from Fat	18	18	18	

Crescia al Formaggio

Crescia is a conjugated form of the Italian verb *crescere,* which means "to grow." This bread, rich in cheese flavor, rises steadily. The cheese in the bread is best melted in the microwave ahead of time so that it adds to the liquidity of the bread during mixing. When the bread is not baked in the bread machine, the cheese is typically folded into the dough before the final rise and bake. Using the bread machine can work too, but as the cheese melts, it adds to the liquidity of the bread, which can cause the loaf to fall from a high rise. That's why it is better to melt the cheese before adding it to the machine.

INGREDIENTS	2-Pound	1 1/2-Pound	1-Pound
warm water	14 ounces	1 1/4 cups	7 ounces
butter	1/2 cup	3/8 cup	4 tablespoons
Swiss cheese (shredded & melted)	2/3 cup	1/2 cup	1/3 cup
sugar	1/2 teaspoon	1/2 teaspoon	1/4 teaspoon
salt	1/2 teaspoon	1/2 teaspoon	1/4 teaspoon
parmesan cheese (grated)	2/3 cup	1/2 cup	1/3 cup
bread flour	3 1/2 cups	2 3/4 cups	1 3/4 cups
active dry yeast	1 tablespoon	2 1/4 teaspoons	1 1/2 teaspoons

NUTRITIONAL ANALYSIS

	2-Pound	1 1/2-Pound	1-Pound	
Total **Calories**	3104	2392	1552	
Total **Protein**	107	82	53	grams
Total **Carbohydrates**	359	282	180	grams
Total **Fat**	136	102	68	grams
Total **Saturated Fat**	81	61	41	grams
Total **Cholesterol**	357	267	178	milligrams
Total **Sodium**	3208	2673	1604	milligrams
Total **Fiber**	15	12	7	grams
% Calories from Fat	40	39	40	

Weissbrot mit Kümmel

White bread with caraway is a favorite in Austria and Germany. It is excellent as a sandwich bread.

INGREDIENTS

1½-Pound		1-Pound
1½ teaspoons	**active dry yeast**	1 teaspoon
2 teaspoons	**caraway seeds**	1½ teaspoons
1½ tablespoons	**sugar**	1 tablespoon
3 cups	**bread flour**	2 cups
2 teaspoons	**salt**	1½ teaspoons
5 tablespoons	**butter**	3 tablespoons
1	**egg**	1
5 ounces	**warm milk**	3 ounces
2 ounces	**warm water**	1½ ounces

NOTES:

1. For Panasonic/National machines, use 3 teaspoons of yeast for the 1½-pound loaf.
2. For DAK/Welbilt machines, use 2 additional tablespoons of warm water for the 1½-pound loaf.

NUTRITIONAL ANALYSIS

	1½-Pound	1-Pound	
Total **Calories**	2217	1467	
Total **Protein**	63	44	grams
Total **Carbohydrates**	328	218	grams
Total **Fat**	71	45	grams
Total **Saturated Fat**	39	24	grams
Total **Cholesterol**	374	310	milligrams
Total **Sodium**	4417	3315	milligrams
Total **Fiber**	7	5	grams
% **Calories from Fat**	29	28	

Danish Sour Bread

This dense, whole-grain bread doesn't rise much. It has a hearty, tart flavor. The rice flour called for is generally available in health-food stores.

INGREDIENTS

1 1/2-Pound		1-Pound
1 1/2 teaspoons	**active dry yeast**	1 teaspoon
3 tablespoons	**gluten (optional)**	2 tablespoons
3/4 cup	**sourdough starter batter**	1/2 cup
1 teaspoon	**ground caraway seed**	1/2 teaspoon
1 teaspoon	**salt**	1/2 teaspoon
1/2 cup	**rice flour**	1/4 cup
1/2 cup	**rye flour**	1/4 cup
2 cups	**whole-wheat flour**	1 1/2 cups
9 ounces	**warm water**	6 ounces
3 tablespoons	**butter**	2 tablespoons

NOTES:

1. For Panasonic/National machines, use 3 teaspoons of yeast for the 1 1/2-pound loaf.
2. For DAK/Welbilt machines, use 2 additional tablespoons of warm water for the 1 1/2-pound loaf.

NUTRITIONAL ANALYSIS

	1 1/2-Pound	1-Pound	
Total **Calories**	1918	1276	
Total **Protein**	65	43	grams
Total **Carbohydrates**	339	226	grams
Total **Fat**	44	29	grams
Total **Saturated Fat**	23	15	grams
Total **Cholesterol**	93	62	milligrams
Total **Sodium**	2142	1073	milligrams
Total **Fiber**	35	25	grams
% **Calories from Fat**	21	21	

Italian Herb Bread

This bread is great with any Italian dish or any salad. It's also good for making salad croutons.

INGREDIENTS	2-Pound	1 1/2-Pound	1-Pound
water	1 1/2 cups	9 ounces	3/4 cup
applesauce	1/4 cup	3 tablespoons	2 tablespoons
honey	2 tablespoons	1 1/2 tablespoons	1 tablespoon
whole-wheat flour	4 cups	3 cups	2 cups
wheat gluten	3 tablespoons	2 1/4 tablespoons	1 1/2 tablespoons
dried onions	1/4 cup	3 tablespoons	2 tablespoons
chives (freeze dried)	1 1/3 tablespoons	1 tablespoon	2 teaspoons
salt	2 teaspoons	1 1/2 teaspoons	1 teaspoon
garlic powder	1 1/2 teaspoons	1 teaspoon	3/4 teaspoon
oregano	1 1/2 teaspoons	1 1/4 teaspoons	3/4 teaspoon
basil	1/2 teaspoon	1/4 teaspoon	1/4 teaspoon
active dry yeast	1 tablespoon	2 1/4 teaspoons	1 1/2 teaspoons

NUTRITIONAL ANALYSIS

	2-Pound	1 1/2-Pound	1-Pound	
Total **Calories**	2095	1571	1048	
Total **Protein**	109	81	54	grams
Total **Carbohydrates**	420	314	210	grams
Total **Fat**	13	10	7	grams
Total **Saturated Fat**	2	2	1	grams
Total **Cholesterol**	0	0	0	milligrams
Total **Sodium**	4375	2181	2188	milligrams
Total **Fiber**	65	49	32	grams
% Calories from Fat	5	5	5	

Finnish Easter-Crown Bread

Traditionally, Finns bake this bread in the spring to celebrate the arrival of the new calves and the abundance of dairy products. It is delicious with cream cheese or other soft, spreadable cheeses.

INGREDIENTS

1½-Pound		1-Pound
1½ teaspoons	**active dry yeast**	1 teaspoon
¾ cup	**rye flour**	½ cup
¼ teaspoon	**dried orange peel**	¼ teaspoon
¼ teaspoon	**dried lemon peel**	¼ teaspoon
½ teaspoon	**cardamom**	½ teaspoon
½ teaspoon	**salt**	½ teaspoon
6 tablespoons	**sugar**	4 tablespoons
2 cups	**all-purpose flour**	1½ cups
1	**egg yolk**	1
4½ tablespoons	**butter**	3 tablespoons
1 ounce	**warm water**	1 ounce
6 ounces	**whipping cream**	4 ounces
4 tablespoons	**chopped almonds**	2½ tablespoons
¼ cup	**raisins**	2 tablespoons

NOTES:

1. For Panasonic/National machines, use 3 teaspoons of yeast for the 1½-pound loaf. For DAK/Welbilt machines, use 2 additional tablespoons of warm water for the 1½-pound loaf.
3. Add the raisins and almonds at the mix-cycle beep or at the end of the initial mix cycle, if your machine is not equipped with an automatic mix cycle.

NUTRITIONAL ANALYSIS

	1½-Pound	1-Pound	
Total **Calories**	2784	1937	
Total **Protein**	65	48	grams
Total **Carbohydrates**	380	265	grams
Total **Fat**	118	80	grams
Total **Saturated Fat**	59	40	grams
Total **Cholesterol**	429	357	milligrams
Total **Sodium**	1241	1203	milligrams
Total **Fiber**	9	6	grams
% **Calories from Fat**	38	37	

Rieska Bread II

This recipe lets you mix the dough in your bread machine and then bake the bread in your oven. The result is an authentically shaped and flavored loaf.

INGREDIENTS

1½-Pound		1-Pound
3 teaspoons	**baking powder**	2 teaspoons
1½ teaspoons	**salt**	1 teaspoon
2 tablespoons	**sugar**	4 teaspoons
3 cups	**barley flour**	2 cups
9 ounces	**cream**	6 ounces
3 tablespoons	**butter**	2 tablespoons

Instructions for baking: Remove the dough from the bread machine after the mixing is completed. Flour your hands and form the dough into a ball. Place the dough ball on a greased cookie sheet and flatten it until it is about ½ inch thick. Use a fork to poke holes in the surface of the dough.

Bake in a preheated, 450-degree/F oven until it is crisp and golden brown. To serve, cut the loaf into wedges while it is still hot. Butter it liberally.

NUTRITIONAL ANALYSIS

	1½-Pound	1-Pound	
Total **Calories**	2147	1431	
Total **Protein**	51	34	grams
Total **Carbohydrates**	245	163	grams
Total **Fat**	94	63	grams
Total **Saturated Fat**	55	37	grams
Total **Cholesterol**	208	139	milligrams
Total **Sodium**	3345	2230	milligrams
Total **Fiber**	43	29	grams
% **Calories from Fat**	40	40	

Olive, Mint, & Onion Bread

This unusual bread originated in Cyprus, where olive trees abound, and stems from the traditional Greek bread called *eliopsomo.*

INGREDIENTS	2-Pound	1½-Pound	1-Pound
water	11 ounces	8½ ounces	5½ ounces
olive oil	2 tablespoons	1½ tablespoons	1 tablespoon
sugar	½ teaspoon	½ teaspoon	¼ teaspoon
whole-wheat flour	½ cup	⅜ cup	¼ cup
bread flour	3 cups	2¼ cups	1½ cups
salt	1 teaspoon	¾ teaspoon	½ teaspoon
dried mint flakes	2 teaspoons	1½ teaspoons	1 teaspoon
onions (chopped)	½ cup	⅜ cup	4 tablespoons
black olives (chopped)	¼ cup	3 tablespoons	2 tablespoons
active dry yeast	2 teaspoons	1½ teaspoons	1 teaspoon

NUTRITIONAL ANALYSIS

	2-Pound	1½-Pound	1-Pound	
Total **Calories**	2012	1511	1006	
Total **Protein**	62	46	31	grams
Total **Carbohydrates**	352	265	176	grams
Total **Fat**	39	29	20	grams
Total **Saturated Fat**	5	4	3	grams
Total **Cholesterol**	0	0	0	milligrams
Total **Sodium**	2747	2061	1374	milligrams
Total **Fiber**	20	15	10	grams
% Calories from Fat	18	18	18	

Suomalaisleipaa Bread

Rye grain grows well in Finland's cold climate. This bread combines rye flour and brown sugar to create a loaf that's deep brown in color. It's great served warm with fresh butter.

INGREDIENTS

1½-Pound		**1-Pound**
1½ teaspoons	**active dry yeast**	1 teaspoon
1¾ cups	**bread flour**	1 cup + 2 tablespoons
1½ teaspoons	**salt**	1 teaspoon
1½ tablespoons	**brown sugar**	1 tablespoon
1½ cups	**rye flour**	1 cup
1 tablespoon	**butter**	½ tablespoon
9 ounces	**warm water**	6 ounces

NOTES:

1. For Panasonic/National machines, use 3 teaspoons of yeast for the 1½-pound loaf.
2. For DAK/Welbilt machines, use 2 additional tablespoons of warm water for the 1½-pound loaf.

NUTRITIONAL ANALYSIS

	1½-Pound	**1-Pound**	
Total **Calories**	1676	1082	
Total **Protein**	57	38	grams
Total **Carbohydrates**	327	215	grams
Total **Fat**	21	12	grams
Total **Saturated Fat**	8	4	grams
Total **Cholesterol**	31	16	milligrams
Total **Sodium**	3213	2142	milligrams
Total **Fiber**	7	5	grams
% Calories from Fat	11	10	

Bohemian Christmas Bread

This delightful bread is great for parties and celebrations. The raisins and nuts give it a festive flavor and texture that's hard to beat. Because this bread is an extremely high riser, a 1-pound loaf will easily fill a large bread-machine bucket. Test the small recipe first to see how the loaf rises in your machine.

INGREDIENTS

1½-Pound		1-Pound
1½ teaspoons	**active dry yeast**	1 teaspoon
3 cups	**bread flour**	2 cups
1 teaspoon	**lemon peel (dried)**	½ teaspoon
1½ teaspoons	**salt**	1 teaspoon
3½ tablespoons	**sugar**	2½ tablespoons
1	**egg**	1
2 tablespoons	**butter**	1½ tablespoons
6 ounces	**warm milk**	½ cup
2 ounces	**warm water**	1½ ounces
4½ tablespoons	**almonds (chopped)**	3 tablespoons
3½ tablespoons	**raisins**	2½ tablespoons

NOTES:

1. For Panasonic/National machines, use 3 teaspoons of yeast for the 1½-pound loaf.
2. If your machine has a mix cycle, the almonds and raisins can be added at the beginning or at the mix beep. They can also be added toward the end of the mixing process.

NUTRITIONAL ANALYSIS

	1½-Pound	1-Pound	
Total **Calories**	2320	1600	
Total **Protein**	69	48	grams
Total **Carbohydrates**	382	258	grams
Total **Fat**	58	42	grams
Total **Saturated Fat**	20	15	grams
Total **Cholesterol**	283	265	milligrams
Total **Sodium**	3371	2268	milligrams
Total **Fiber**	10	7	grams
% **Calories from Fat**	22	24	

Pusstabrot

Hungarian white bread is light and airy. The fennel and garlic give it a great flavor. It is an excellent sandwich bread.

INGREDIENTS

1 1/2-Pound		1-Pound
1 1/2 teaspoons	**active dry yeast**	1 teaspoon
3 cups	**bread flour**	2 cups
1/2 teaspoon	**garlic salt**	1/2 teaspoon
1 teaspoon	**salt**	1/2 teaspoon
1/4 teaspoon	**fennel seed**	1/8 teaspoon
5 1/2 teaspoons	**sugar**	4 teaspoons
1 1/2 tablespoons	**olive oil**	1 tablespoon
9 ounces	**warm water**	6 ounces

NOTE:
For Panasonic/National machines, use 3 teaspoons of yeast for the 1 1/2-pound loaf.

NUTRITIONAL ANALYSIS

	1 1/2-Pound	1-Pound	
Total **Calories**	1758	1177	
Total **Protein**	51	34	grams
Total **Carbohydrates**	321	216	grams
Total **Fat**	27	18	grams
Total **Saturated Fat**	4	2	grams
Total **Cholesterol**	0	0	milligrams
Total **Sodium**	3206	2137	milligrams
Total **Fiber**	7	4	grams
% **Calories from Fat**	14	14	

Babovka

This sweet, lightly textured Czech bread is best served hot, sprinkled with a mixture of powdered sugar and cinnamon.

INGREDIENTS

1 1/2-Pound		1-Pound
1 teaspoon	**active dry yeast**	1/2 teaspoon
3 cups	**bread flour**	2 cups
1/2 teaspoon	**salt**	1/4 teaspoon
5 tablespoons	**brown sugar**	3 tablespoons
7 ounces	**warm milk**	5 ounces
2	**egg yolks**	1
5 tablespoons	**butter**	3 tablespoons
1/2 cup	**raisins**	1/3 cup

NOTES:

1. For machines with yeast dispensers, use 2 teaspoons of yeast for the 1 1/2-pound loaf.
2. Raisins can be added at the mix-cycle beep, if your machine is so equipped.

NUTRITIONAL ANALYSIS

	1 1/2-Pound	1-Pound	
Total **Calories**	2203	1428	
Total **Protein**	72	46	grams
Total **Carbohydrates**	434	285	grams
Total **Fat**	20	11	grams
Total **Saturated Fat**	6	3	grams
Total **Cholesterol**	435	219	milligrams
Total **Sodium**	1336	695	milligrams
Total **Fiber**	10	7	grams
% **Calories from Fat**	8	7	

Cuban Bread

Corn, the staple grain of Latin America, is the featured ingredient in this light and tasty bread. It is excellent with any Latin American dish and with foods from the American Southwest. The bread has a somewhat salty taste, so if you'd like less salt, feel free to cut down on the amount of it.

INGREDIENTS

1½-Pound		1-Pound
1½ teaspoons	**active dry yeast**	1 teaspoon
1 tablespoon	**cornmeal**	½ tablespoon
3 cups	**all-purpose flour**	2 cups
2 teaspoons	**salt**	1½ teaspoons
½ tablespoon	**sugar**	1 teaspoon
9 ounces	**warm water**	6 ounces

NOTE:
For Panasonic/National machines, use 3 teaspoons of yeast for the 1½-pound loaf.

NUTRITIONAL ANALYSIS

	1½-Pound	1-Pound	
Total **Calories**	1546	1026	
Total **Protein**	51	34	grams
Total **Carbohydrates**	311	207	grams
Total **Fat**	7	5	grams
Total **Saturated Fat**	1	1	grams
Total **Cholesterol**	0	0	milligrams
Total **Sodium**	4275	3205	milligrams
Total **Fiber**	7	5	grams
% **Calories from Fat**	4	4	

English Oatmeal Bread

Oatmeal and whole-wheat flour make this a tasty loaf. It's a great variation on white bread, yet the whole-grain flavors aren't overpowering.

INGREDIENTS

1½-Pound		1-Pound
2 teaspoons	**active dry yeast**	1½ teaspoons
1½ cups	**bread flour**	1 cup
½ cup	**whole-wheat flour**	¼ cup
1½ teaspoons	**salt**	1 teaspoon
1 cup	**rolled oats**	¾ cup
3 tablespoons	**butter**	2 tablespoons
3 ounces	**warm water**	2 ounces
7 ounces	**warm milk**	5 ounces

NOTES:

1. For Panasonic/National machines, use 3½ teaspoons of yeast for the 1½-pound loaf.
2. For DAK/Welbilt machines, use 2 additional tablespoons of warm water for the 1½-pound loaf.

NUTRITIONAL ANALYSIS

	1½-Pound	1-Pound	
Total **Calories**	1660	1104	
Total **Protein**	55	37	grams
Total **Carbohydrates**	259	170	grams
Total **Fat**	46	31	grams
Total **Saturated Fat**	24	16	grams
Total **Cholesterol**	102	68	milligrams
Total **Sodium**	3318	2217	milligrams
Total **Fiber**	20	13	grams
% **Calories from Fat**	25	25	

Irish Barmbrack

Although it doesn't rise much, this dense loaf is very sweet and quite tasty. Barmbrack ("yeast bread") is one of the rare examples of yeast being used in traditional Irish baking.

INGREDIENTS

1 1/2-Pound		1-Pound
1 1/2 teaspoons	**active dry yeast**	1 teaspoon
3/4 teaspoon	**lemon peel (dried)**	1/2 teaspoon
3/4 teaspoon	**allspice**	1/2 teaspoon
1 1/2 teaspoons	**salt**	1 teaspoon
3/4 cup	**sugar**	1/2 cup
3 cups	**bread flour**	2 cups
3 1/2 tablespoons	**butter**	2 1/2 tablespoons
2 ounces	**warm water**	1 ounce
6 ounces	**warm milk**	1/2 cup
6 tablespoons	**seedless raisins**	1/4 cup
6 tablespoons	**currants**	1/4 cup

NOTES:

1. For Panasonic/National machines, use 3 teaspoons of yeast for the 1 1/2-pound loaf.
2. Raisins and currants may be added in the beginning or at the mix beep (if your machine is equipped with one).

NUTRITIONAL ANALYSIS

	1 1/2-Pound	1-Pound	
Total **Calories**	2765	1883	
Total **Protein**	60	40	grams
Total **Carbohydrates**	528	358	grams
Total **Fat**	49	35	grams
Total **Saturated Fat**	27	19	grams
Total **Cholesterol**	116	83	milligrams
Total **Sodium**	3314	2210	milligrams
Total **Fiber**	12	8	grams
% **Calories from Fat**	16	17	

Yorkshire Spice Bread

A raisin-bread lover's favorite, this makes an excellent breakfast bread.

INGREDIENTS

1½-Pound		1-Pound
1½ teaspoons	**active dry yeast**	1 teaspoon
½ teaspoon	**cinnamon**	½ teaspoon
2½ cups + 2 tablespoons	**bread flour**	1¾ cups
½ teaspoon	**nutmeg**	½ teaspoon
1 tablespoon	**dried orange peel**	2 teaspoons
½ cup	**sugar**	5 tablespoons
1	**egg**	1
2 tablespoons	**olive oil**	4 teaspoons
3 tablespoons	**butter**	2 tablespoons
½ tablespoon	**maple syrup**	1 teaspoon
¾ cup	**warm milk**	½ cup
½ cup	**raisins**	¼ cup

NOTES:

1. For Panasonic/National machines, use 3 teaspoons of yeast for the 1½-pound loaf.
2. You may add the raisins at the beginning or at the mix beep (if your machine has one).

NUTRITIONAL ANALYSIS

	1½-Pound	1-Pound	
Total **Calories**	2485	1637	
Total **Protein**	60	41	grams
Total **Carbohydrates**	397	253	grams
Total **Fat**	75	52	grams
Total **Saturated Fat**	29	20	grams
Total **Cholesterol**	314	280	milligrams
Total **Sodium**	180	140	milligrams
Total **Fiber**	10	6	grams
% **Calories from Fat**	27	28	

TRADITIONAL BREADS

These breads have their roots in the American past and are traditional favorites in various parts of the United States.

Bacon-Cheese Bread

A wonderful variation on white bread that has a moist texture and is great for sandwiches. You can use bacon or cheese substitutes in lieu of the real thing. The nutritional analysis doesn't include the cheese or bacon, since that varies according to the type you use.

INGREDIENTS	2-Pound	1½-Pound	1-Pound
milk	1⅓ cups	1 cup	⅔ cup
butter	2 tablespoons	1⅓ tablespoons	1 tablespoon
sugar	1⅓ tablespoons	1 tablespoon	2 teaspoons
salt	1 teaspoon	½ teaspoon	½ teaspoon
bread flour	4 cups	3 cups	2 cups
active dry yeast	2 teaspoons	1½ teaspoons	1 teaspoon
	Add at mix cycle:		
cheddar cheese (shredded)	½ cup	6 tablespoons	¼ cup
cooked bacon (crumbled)	½ cup	6 tablespoons	¼ cup

NUTRITIONAL ANALYSIS

	2-Pound	1½-Pound	1-Pound	
Total **Calories**	2467	1834	1233	
Total **Protein**	80	60	40	grams
Total **Carbohydrates**	432	324	216	grams
Total **Fat**	43	30	22	grams
Total **Saturated Fat**	22	16	11	grams
Total **Cholesterol**	106	74	53	milligrams
Total **Sodium**	2538	1351	1269	milligrams
Total **Fiber**	4	3	2	grams
% **Calories from Fat**	16	15	16	

Blue Ribbon Potato Bread

Here is a simple loaf of potato bread that has very few ingredients to round up, is quick to put together, and is very tasty.

INGREDIENTS	2-Pound	1½-Pound	1-Pound
warm water	1⅓ cups	1 cup	⅔ cup
salt	2 teaspoons	1½ teaspoons	1 teaspoon
butter	1⅓ tablespoons	1½ tablespoons	2½ teaspoons
potato flakes	3⅓ tablespoons	2½ tablespoons	5 teaspoons
sugar	2 tablespoons	1½ tablespoons	1 tablespoon
bread flour	4 cups	3 cups	2 cups
active dry yeast	2 teaspoons	1½ teaspoons	1 teaspoon

NUTRITIONAL ANALYSIS

	2-Pound	1½-Pound	1-Pound	
Total **Calories**	2299	1749	1150	
Total **Protein**	70	52	35	grams
Total **Carbohydrates**	433	325	217	grams
Total **Fat**	28	24	14	grams
Total **Saturated Fat**	13	12	7	grams
Total **Cholesterol**	51	46	26	milligrams
Total **Sodium**	4491	3397	2245	milligrams
Total **Fiber**	16	12	8	grams
% **Calories from Fat**	11	13	11	

Colonial Bread

This traditional bread uses ingredients that were commonly found on the colonial farm and has a crunchy texture unique to recipes containing cornmeal.

INGREDIENTS	2-Pound	1½-Pound	1-Pound
warm water	1½ cups	9 ounces	6 ounces
molasses	⅓ cup	3⅓ tablespoons	2½ tablespoons
butter	3 tablespoons	2⅓ tablespoons	1½ tablespoons
yellow cornmeal	⅓ cup	3¾ tablespoons	2½ tablespoons
salt	1 teaspoon	¾ teaspoon	½ teaspoon
bread flour	3½ cups	2⅝ cups	1¾ cups
active dry yeast	1½ teaspoons	1¼ teaspoons	¾ teaspoon

NUTRITIONAL ANALYSIS

	2-Pound	1½-Pound	1-Pound	
Total **Calories**	2504	1847	1240	
Total **Protein**	64	48	32	grams
Total **Carbohydrates**	460	335	227	grams
Total **Fat**	43	33	22	grams
Total **Saturated Fat**	23	18	11	grams
Total **Cholesterol**	92	71	46	milligrams
Total **Sodium**	2543	1912	1270	milligrams
Total **Fiber**	7	5	3	grams
% **Calories from Fat**	16	16	16	

Eleanor Roosevelt's Whole-Wheat Bread

This recipe was adapted from *The White House Cookbook* (Culinary Arts Institute, Chicago, Illinois, 1968). Mrs. Franklin D. Roosevelt liked wheat bread and served it at many White House gatherings. She enjoyed coarse bread and liked to use fresh stone-ground whole-wheat flour.

INGREDIENTS	2-Pound	1½-Pound	1-Pound
molasses	¼ cup	3 tablespoons	2 tablespoons
butter	1 tablespoon	1 tablespoon	½ tablespoon
warm water	1½ cups	1 cup	6 ounces
whole-wheat flour	1 cup	¾ cup	½ cup
brown sugar	1 tablespoon	2¼ teaspoons	½ tablespoon
salt	1 teaspoon	¾ teaspoon	½ teaspoon
bread flour	3½ cups	2⅝ cups	1¾ cups
active dry yeast	2 teaspoons	1½ teaspoons	1 teaspoon

NUTRITIONAL ANALYSIS

	2-Pound	1½-Pound	1-Pound	
Total **Calories**	2514	1911	1257	
Total **Protein**	77	58	39	grams
Total **Carbohydrates**	503	377	252	grams
Total **Fat**	22	19	11	grams
Total **Saturated Fat**	9	8	4	grams
Total **Cholesterol**	31	31	15	milligrams
Total **Sodium**	2312	1762	1156	milligrams
Total **Fiber**	28	21	14	grams
% **Calories from Fat**	8	9	8	

Farmer Bread

A traditional white loaf made sweeter by dates and nuts.

INGREDIENTS	2-Pound	1½-Pound	1-Pound
eggs	2	1	1
butter	3/8 cup	1/4 cup	3 tablespoons
milk	10 ounces	8 ounces	5 ounces
walnuts (chopped)	1/4 cup	3 tablespoons	2 tablespoons
dates (chopped)	1/4 cup	3 tablespoons	2 tablespoons
salt	2 teaspoons	1½ teaspoons	1 teaspoon
bread flour	4 cups	3 cups	2 cups
sugar	3 tablespoons	2½ tablespoons	1½ tablespoons
lemon peel	1 tablespoon	2¼ teaspoons	1½ teaspoons
active dry yeast	2 teaspoons	1½ teaspoons	1 teaspoon

NUTRITIONAL ANALYSIS

	2-Pound	1½-Pound	1-Pound	
Total **Calories**	3205	2343	1603	
Total **Protein**	92	67	46	grams
Total **Carbohydrates**	484	366	242	grams
Total **Fat**	100	68	50	grams
Total **Saturated Fat**	53	36	26	grams
Total **Cholesterol**	584	334	292	milligrams
Total **Sodium**	5221	3838	2610	milligrams
Total **Fiber**	19	15	10	grams
% **Calories from Fat**	28	26	28	

Honey-Barley Bread

The distinctive flavor of barley is evident in this bread that combines three different types of flour.

INGREDIENTS	2-Pound	1 1/2-Pound	1-Pound
warm water	2 cups	1 1/2 cups	1 cup
honey	1/3 cup	1/4 cup	2 1/2 tablespoons
wheat gluten	1/4 cup	3 tablespoons	2 tablespoons
bread flour	2 1/3 cups	1 3/4 cups	1 1/8 cups
barley flour	2/3 cup	1/2 cup	1/3 cup
salt	1 teaspoon	1/2 teaspoon	1/2 teaspoon
whole-wheat flour	1 1/2 cups	1 1/4 cups	3/4 cup
active dry yeast	1 tablespoon	2 teaspoons	1 1/2 teaspoons

NUTRITIONAL ANALYSIS

	2-Pound	1 1/2-Pound	1-Pound	
Total **Calories**	2361	1834	1181	
Total **Protein**	115	88	58	grams
Total **Carbohydrates**	457	358	229	grams
Total **Fat**	13	10	7	grams
Total **Saturated Fat**	2	2	1	grams
Total **Cholesterol**	0	0	0	milligrams
Total **Sodium**	2256	1159	1128	milligrams
Total **Fiber**	27	22	27	grams
% Calories from Fat	5	5	5	

Mormon Rye Bread

A traditional recipe from the 19th century, modernized to include yeast as leavening.

INGREDIENTS	2-Pound	1½-Pound	1-Pound
warm water	7 ounces	5½ ounces	3½ ounces
honey	¼ cup	3 tablespoons	2 tablespoons
shortening	½ cup	⅜ cup	4 tablespoons
butter	2 tablespoons	1½ tablespoons	1 tablespoon
sugar	1 tablespoon	2¼ teaspoons	½ teaspoon
rye flour	1 cup	¾ cup	½ cup
bread flour	3 cups	2¼ cups	1½ cups
brown sugar	¼ cup	3 tablespoons	2 tablespoons
salt	1 teaspoon	¾ teaspoon	½ teaspoon
active dry yeast	1 tablespoon	2½ teaspoons	1½ teaspoons

NUTRITIONAL ANALYSIS

	2-Pound	1½-Pound	1-Pound	
Total **Calories**	3429	2575	1715	
Total **Protein**	64	48	32	grams
Total **Carbohydrates**	499	375	250	grams
Total **Fat**	134	101	67	grams
Total **Saturated Fat**	41	31	21	grams
Total **Cholesterol**	61	46	31	milligrams
Total **Sodium**	2404	1804	1202	milligrams
Total **Fiber**	28	22	14	grams
% Calories from Fat	35	35	35	

Mountain Rye Bread

This basic recipe will give you the taste of rye with a fluffy consistency.

INGREDIENTS	2-Pound	$1^1/_2$-Pound	1-Pound
warm water	2 cups	$1^1/_2$ cups	1 cup
vegetable oil	2 tablespoons	$1^1/_2$ tablespoons	1 tablespoon
honey	$^1/_2$ cup	3 tablespoons	2 tablespoons
salt	2 teaspoons	$1^1/_2$ teaspoons	1 teaspoon
caraway seed	2 tablespoons	$1^1/_2$ tablespoons	1 tablespoon
rye flour	2 cups	$1^1/_2$ cups	1 cup
bread flour	$3^1/_2$ cups	$2^1/_2$ cups	$1^3/_4$ cups
nonfat dry milk	$^3/_8$ cup	$^1/_4$ cup	3 tablespoons
active dry yeast	1 tablespoon	$2^1/_4$ teaspoons	$1^1/_2$ teaspoons

NUTRITIONAL ANALYSIS

	2-Pound	$1^1/_2$-Pound	1-Pound	
Total **Calories**	3194	2334	1597	
Total **Protein**	100	73	50	grams
Total **Carbohydrates**	610	445	305	grams
Total **Fat**	42	31	21	grams
Total **Saturated Fat**	5	4	3	grams
Total **Cholesterol**	9	7	4	milligrams
Total **Sodium**	4544	3407	2272	milligrams
Total **Fiber**	13	9	6	grams
% **Calories from Fat**	12	12	12	

Mustard Grain Bread

This whole-grain bread features 3 different types of flour and the tang of Dijon mustard.

INGREDIENTS	2-Pound	1 1/2-Pound	1-Pound
warm water	1 cup	3/4 cup	1/2 cup
butter	1/4 cup	3 tablespoons	2 tablespoons
Dijon mustard	2/3 cup	1/2 cup	1/3 cup
sugar	2 teaspoons	1 1/2 teaspoons	1 teaspoon
salt	1 teaspoon	1 teaspoon	1/2 teaspoon
bread flour	1 1/2 cups	1 1/3 cups	3/4 cup
rye flour	3/4 cup	2/3 cup	1/2 cup
whole-wheat flour	1 cup	2/3 cup	1/2 cup
active dry yeast	1 1/2 tablespoons	3 teaspoons	2 teaspoons

NUTRITIONAL ANALYSIS

	2-Pound	1 1/2-Pound	1-Pound	
Total **Calories**	2026	1622	1014	
Total **Protein**	63	50	31	grams
Total **Carbohydrates**	321	262	161	grams
Total **Fat**	60	46	30	grams
Total **Saturated Fat**	30	22	15	grams
Total **Cholesterol**	123	92	61	milligrams
Total **Sodium**	4626	4002	2313	milligrams
Total **Fiber**	24	17	11	grams
% **Calories from Fat**	26	25	26	

Nutmeg Bread

Try this bread for a spicy treat. Excellent as toast.

INGREDIENTS	2-Pound	1½-Pound	1-Pound
warm water	1⅓ cups	1 cup	⅔ cup
eggs	2	1	1
orange juice	2 tablespoons	1½ tablespoons	1 tablespoon
honey	3⅓ tablespoons	2½ tablespoons	1⅔ tablespoons
salt	½ teaspoon	¼ teaspoon	1 to 3 dashes
nutmeg	¾ teaspoon	½ teaspoon	⅓ teaspoon
whole-wheat flour	4½ cups	3⅓ cups	2¼ cups
active dry yeast	2 teaspoons	1½ teaspoons	1 teaspoon

NUTRITIONAL ANALYSIS

	2-Pound	1½-Pound	1-Pound	
Total **Calories**	2283	1694	1120	
Total **Protein**	91	67	45	grams
Total **Carbohydrates**	469	348	232	grams
Total **Fat**	21	16	11	grams
Total **Saturated Fat**	5	4	3	grams
Total **Cholesterol**	425	319	213	milligrams
Total **Sodium**	1237	661	440	milligrams
Total **Fiber**	69	51	34	grams
% **Calories from Fat**	8	8	8	

Parsley Bread

Try this bread for a variation on the white-bread theme. The parsley and garlic add zest to this tasty bread.

INGREDIENTS	2-Pound	1 1/2-Pound	1-Pound
warm water	1 3/4 cups	1 1/4 cups	7 ounces
olive oil	2 tablespoons	1 1/2 tablespoons	1 tablespoon
parsley (chopped)	2 2/3 tablespoons	2 tablespoons	4 teaspoons
minced garlic	1 teaspoon	1 teaspoon	1/2 teaspoon
sugar	2 tablespoons	1 1/2 tablespoons	1 tablespoon
wheat bran	1/4 cup	3 tablespoons	2 tablespoons
wheat germ	1/4 cup	3 tablespoons	2 tablespoons
bread flour	4 cups	3 cups	2 cups
active dry yeast	2 teaspoons	1 1/2 teaspoons	1 teaspoon

NUTRITIONAL ANALYSIS

	2-Pound	1 1/2-Pound	1-Pound	
Total **Calories**	2487	1866	1244	
Total **Protein**	79	59	39	grams
Total **Carbohydrates**	453	340	226	grams
Total **Fat**	40	30	20	grams
Total **Saturated Fat**	6	4	3	grams
Total **Cholesterol**	0	0	0	milligrams
Total **Sodium**	48	35	24	milligrams
Total **Fiber**	11	8	6	grams
% **Calories from Fat**	15	15	15	

Polenta, Millet & Sunflower Seed Bread

When my boys were small, they planted some sunflower seeds in our backyard in Arizona. To their amazement, the plants grew over 10 feet tall, and had a large sunflower at the top of each stalk. Sunflower seeds are native to the American Southwest and to Mexico, and have become very popular in American baking. This bread is a wonderful blend of grains with cornmeal, millet, and whole wheat. (Polenta is actually an Italian mush that is sometimes made from cornmeal.) There is enough bread flour to give the bread a wonderful, smooth texture that makes it excellent for toasting.

INGREDIENTS	2-Pound	1½-Pound	1-Pound
warm water	1 cup	¾ cup	½ cup
honey	¼ cup	3 tablespoons	2 tablespoons
vegetable oil	2 tablespoons	1½ tablespoons	1 tablespoon
eggs	2	1	1
sugar	½ teaspoon	½ teaspoon	¼ teaspoon
salt	1 teaspoon	¾ teaspoon	½ teaspoon
raw millet	¼ cup	3 tablespoons	2 tablespoons
cornmeal	¼ cup	3 tablespoons	2 tablespoons
whole-wheat flour	1 cup	¾ cup	½ cup
bread flour	2½ cups	2 cups	1¼ cups
sunflower seeds	¼ cup	3 tablespoons	2 tablespoons
active dry yeast	2 teaspoons	1½ teaspoons	1 teaspoon

NUTRITIONAL ANALYSIS

	2-Pound	1½-Pound	1-Pound	
Total **Calories**	2609	1989	1304	
Total **Protein**	81	60	40	grams
Total **Carbohydrates**	456	355	228	grams
Total **Fat**	55	39	27	grams
Total **Saturated Fat**	8	6	4	grams
Total **Cholesterol**	361	181	181	milligrams
Total **Sodium**	2269	1675	1135	milligrams
Total **Fiber**	31	23	15	grams
% **Calories from Fat**	19	18	19	

Potica

This traditional bread is a smoothly textured sweet white bread that is excellent for breakfast.

INGREDIENTS	2-Pound	1½-Pound	1-Pound
milk	⅜ cup	⅓ cup	3½ tablespoons
shortening	¼ cup	3 tablespoons	2 tablespoons
warm water	⅓ cup	3¾ tablespoons	2½ tablespoons
eggs	2	1	1
butter	¼ cup	3 tablespoons	2 tablespoons
sugar	¼ cup	3 tablespoons	2 tablespoons
walnuts (chopped)	¼ cup	3 tablespoons	2 tablespoons
orange peel (grated)	1 tablespoon	2 teaspoons	½ tablespoon
active dry yeast	1 tablespoon	2 teaspoons	1½ teaspoons

NUTRITIONAL ANALYSIS

	2-Pound	1½-Pound	1-Pound	
Total **Calories**	1312	957	661	
Total **Protein**	21	13	11	grams
Total **Carbohydrates**	62	47	32	grams
Total **Fat**	113	83	57	grams
Total **Saturated Fat**	46	34	23	grams
Total **Cholesterol**	496	284	249	milligrams
Total **Sodium**	624	447	316	milligrams
Total **Fiber**	4	3	2	grams
% **Calories from Fat**	75	76	75	

Pueblo Sage Bread

Since sage grows wild in the Pueblo country of New Mexico, it is a popular herb among the Native Americans of the area. This bread uses some modern ingredients, but has the age-old flavor unique to Southwestern cooking.

INGREDIENTS	2-Pound	1½-Pound	1-Pound
warm water	¼ cup	3 tablespoons	2 tablespoons
cooking oil	2 tablespoons	1½ tablespoons	1 tablespoon
cottage cheese	1 cup	¾ cup	½ cup
eggs	2	1	1
bread flour	3½ cups	2½ cups	1¾ cups
sugar	1 tablespoon	2¼ teaspoons	1½ teaspoons
dried sage	1⅓ tablespoons	1 tablespoon	2 teaspoons
salt	½ teaspoon	½ teaspoon	¼ teaspoon
baking soda	1 teaspoon	¾ teaspoon	½ teaspoon
active dry yeast	1 tablespoon	2¼ teaspoons	1½ teaspoons

NUTRITIONAL ANALYSIS

	2-Pound	1½-Pound	1-Pound	
Total **Calories**	2393	1702	1197	
Total **Protein**	104	73	52	grams
Total **Carbohydrates**	376	269	188	grams
Total **Fat**	49	34	25	grams
Total **Saturated Fat**	10	7	5	grams
Total **Cholesterol**	380	195	190	milligrams
Total **Sodium**	3367	2764	1683	milligrams
Total **Fiber**	15	11	8	grams
% **Calories from Fat**	19	18	19	

Sesame-Honey Bread

Sesame seeds always add a nutty flavor to bread, and this is no exception. It is great toasted with jam or jelly.

INGREDIENTS	2-Pound	1½-Pound	1-Pound
warm water	1⅓ cups	1 cup	⅔ cup
honey	⅓ cup	¼ cup	2½ tablespoons
buttermilk	⅓ cup	¼ cup	2½ tablespoons
salt	2 teaspoons	1½ teaspoons	1 teaspoon
bread flour	4 cups	3 cups	2 cups
wheat flour	¼ cup	3 tablespoons	2 tablespoons
sesame seeds	⅔ cup	½ cup	⅓ cup
active dry yeast	1 tablespoon	2¼ teaspoons	1½ teaspoons

NUTRITIONAL ANALYSIS

	2-Pound	1½-Pound	1-Pound	
Total **Calories**	2948	2229	1474	
Total **Protein**	92	69	46	grams
Total **Carbohydrates**	525	398	262	grams
Total **Fat**	58	44	29	grams
Total **Saturated Fat**	9	7	5	grams
Total **Cholesterol**	3	2	1	milligrams
Total **Sodium**	4385	3293	2193	milligrams
Total **Fiber**	7	6	4	grams
% **Calories from Fat**	18	17	18	

Shaker Daily Loaf

The story goes that a 19th-century Kentucky Shaker community member named Sister Virginia originated this bread and baked it daily. Her original recipe yielded roughly 5 pounds of bread and has, of course, been scaled down for the bread machine. This simple but tasty white bread is an excellent staple white bread, fit for putting on the table while still hot.

INGREDIENTS	2-Pound	1½-Pound	1-Pound
warm water	6 ounces	4½ ounces	3 ounces
milk	⅔ cup	½ cup	⅓ cup
shortening	3 tablespoons	2¼ tablespoons	1½ tablespoons
sugar	2 teaspoons	1½ teaspoons	1 teaspoon
salt	1 teaspoon	¾ teaspoon	½ teaspoon
bread flour	4 cups	3 cups	2 cups
active dry yeast	2 teaspoons	1½ teaspoons	1 teaspoon

NUTRITIONAL ANALYSIS

	2-Pound	1½-Pound	1-Pound	
Total **Calories**	2474	1855	1237	
Total **Protein**	74	56	37	grams
Total **Carbohydrates**	416	312	208	grams
Total **Fat**	53	40	27	grams
Total **Saturated Fat**	14	11	7	grams
Total **Cholesterol**	22	17	11	milligrams
Total **Sodium**	2232	1674	1116	milligrams
Total **Fiber**	15	12	8	grams
% Calories from Fat	20	20	20	

Trail Bread

Rye is a popular grain throughout the world because it will grow in many places where less rugged grains will not. It requires less water than wheat and can grow well in soil of much poorer quality. It was first cultivated in Roman times and quickly became a staple in breads throughout Europe, including Scandinavia and Russia. Since rye is naturally low in gluten content, it doesn't rise much. While the original bread tends to be much denser, for the bread machine we have tried to capture the essence of this bread, although we added more wheat flour to give it a better rise. Substituting rye flour for wheat will work, but take care not to overburden the mixing motor of your bread machine with too dense a loaf.

INGREDIENTS	2-Pound	1½-Pound	1-Pound
warm water	1 cup	¾ cup	½ cup
vegetable oil	3 tablespoons	2¼ tablespoons	1½ tablespoons
honey	2 tablespoons	1½ tablespoons	1 tablespoon
butter	1 tablespoon	2 teaspoons	½ tablespoon
brown sugar	2 tablespoons	1½ tablespoons	1 tablespoon
whole-wheat flour	1 cup	¾ cup	½ cup
bread flour	2 cups	1½ cups	1 cup
rye flour	½ cup	⅜ cup	¼ cup
instant dry milk	¼ cup	3 tablespoons	2 tablespoons
salt	1½ teaspoons	1 teaspoon	¾ cup
raisins	2 tablespoons	1½ tablespoons	1 tablespoon
active dry yeast	1 tablespoon	2¼ teaspoons	1½ teaspoons

NUTRITIONAL ANALYSIS

	2-Pound	1½-Pound	1-Pound	
Total **Calories**	2386	1781	1193	
Total **Protein**	65	49	33	grams
Total **Carbohydrates**	406	304	203	grams
Total **Fat**	61	45	30	grams
Total **Saturated Fat**	13	9	7	grams
Total **Cholesterol**	34	23	17	milligrams
Total **Sodium**	3444	2307	1722	milligrams
Total **Fiber**	33	25	16	grams
% **Calories from Fat**	23	22	23	

Texas Bran Bread

This traditional basic bread has a hint of sweetness and a soft bran texture.

INGREDIENTS	2-Pound	1½-Pound	1-Pound
warm water	1½ cups	9 ounces	6 ounces
butter	3 tablespoons	2 tablespoons	1½ tablespoons
molasses	1 teaspoon	¾ teaspoon	½ teaspoon
brown sugar	2 tablespoons	1½ tablespoons	1 tablespoon
salt	1 teaspoon	¾ teaspoon	½ teaspoon
bread flour	4 cups	3 cups	2 cups
bran	3 tablespoons	2 tablespoons	1½ tablespoons
active dry yeast	2 teaspoons	1½ teaspoons	1 teaspoon

NUTRITIONAL ANALYSIS

	2-Pound	1½-Pound	1-Pound	
Total **Calories**	2414	1783	1207	
Total **Protein**	71	53	35	grams
Total **Carbohydrates**	430	322	215	grams
Total **Fat**	44	30	22	grams
Total **Saturated Fat**	23	15	11	grams
Total **Cholesterol**	92	61	46	milligrams
Total **Sodium**	2514	1856	1257	milligrams
Total **Fiber**	20	15	10	grams
% **Calories from Fat**	17	15	17	

INDEX